This is me

Danny Wilks

Intro

I'm writing this book to tell you my story of an adventure. I am not a writer and will never pretend to be.

Prior to this I had only written about 500 words on any one subject in my entire life. I could probably give you a list the length of my arm of teachers who would testify to this! They would also testify that it was the most smudged incomprehensible mess they had ever tried to read.

However, there is a story in my head that needs to come out so I'm going to do the best job I can, as I feel a bit selfish being the full stories only owner. People ask questions about my journey all the time, but condensing 10 weeks into a quick conversation doesn't do it justice. So the book seems like the best way to get it out.

However, this is not a story about cutting off body parts to survive, or hallucinating your last days on a bus after eating poisonous plants. Nothing is jazzed up; it's just a guy on a quest to get to Alaska, who believes, as my Uncle Dod used to always say, "where there's a will there's a way." And his favourite "Blood Muscle Skin and Bone" which he would refer to when I thought I couldn't do something that others could. At the end of the day everybody is made of blood, muscle, skin and bone so there are no excuses for believing you can't do something because someone else appears to be special.

Chapter one
The Lion the Witch and the Wardrobe

After my first experience with kayaking you would
think I would never set foot in another kayak again,
let alone kayak more than a thousand miles to Alaska.
I'm from a small town in the Scottish Borders called
Earlston. At the time of my first kayak experience I
was living in Galashiels near the River Tweed. I was
working with my mate Alec in a painting and shot
blasting company based further down the Tweed
about six miles by road. I had this great idea that I
could kayak to work!
I was taking the bus to work at the time and thought
kayaking would be a novel and a very cool way to get
to work.
When I told Alec of my idea he was sceptical to say
the least, and pointed out that the Tweed was fast
flowing and there would be no way of transporting it
back every night. However, I'm a bit of a dreamer
and very stubborn. Even if it was no good for getting
to work kayaking would still be a great hobby.
I found a guy selling a white-water kayak for 90
Pounds in Edinburgh and managed to convince Alec
to help me collect it. Being the country bumpkins
that we were, on the way home we got a bit lost and
had to give an old drunk a lift home with the promise
of directions to the main road, but mission
accomplished. The Langlee area of Galashiels is not

really a place where you can walk down the street with a kayak on your shoulder without getting a lot of strange looks! People in Langlee thought that going to the pub in the next town was an adventure! But strange looks weren't going to stop me. Off I went down the Tweed to test it out one Saturday, no life jacket, helmet or experience. Needless to say it didn't go well!   I got into the kayak alright, but as soon as I hit fast moving water I was over capsized brushing my head on a rock. The water was cold and it was a strange feeling being upside down and moving in fast water. I managed to get myself out of the kayak and when I popped up to the surface, the kayak and paddle were within grabbing distance. Getting to the bank was no problem; although the water was fast, it was only waist deep and I guided the kayak in and sat on the rocks with water up my nose, a bit shaken up. It gave me a real scare; more than I would like to admit. The next time I saw Alec and told him what happened he laughed a lot and has taken great pleasure in retelling the story for years afterwards. To this day it still brings out an evil giggle in him. It's worse now as his partner Andrea laughs just as hard and I'm sure they're going to pass the story on to the kids. The part they laugh at the hardest is the fact I actually believed I could get to work in it. The kayak sat in the garden for the rest of its life apart from my friend Nigel taking it out once or twice, and him announcing what a great kayak it was. Eventually it ended up getting hauled halfway over a fence and used as a see saw by the local Langlee kids!

Fast forward 14 years and I'm in Nova Scotia, I

had signed up to a volunteer sight called WWOOF and was helping on a wee hobby farm called the Harrison Lewis Coastal Discovery Centre. It's on the Atlantic Coast around 100 miles (160k) south of Halifax, Sandy Bay.

Annie and Dirk own and run the farm/centre and you couldn't meet two better people. It was awesome; Dirk and Annie published four rural magazines along with running the farm and discovery centre. It was a workload I was extremely impressed with.

There were rural living workshops and university programs, and at the time there was an archaeology team studying an old First Nations midden. The First Nations people had been dumping the seashells in the same place for hundreds of years. The archaeologists even found a human jawbone in one of the excavations. They were worried the site would be closed down but got a ceremonial smudging done to purify, cleanse and repel any spiritual influence and it was all good.

Wwoof is a program where you exchange about four or five hours work a day five days a week for lodging and meals. It's a great way to travel and meet interesting people away from the touristy thing; most countries around the world have their own wwoof site. I went from staying in a hostel to having my own boathouse in the woods by the ocean with some amazing cooking thrown in, all for just a few hours of fun work a day! I was surrounded by some intelligent, hardworking, interesting people. After working in construction where I'm usually surrounded by big kids telling bad jokes all day this was great.

It was my first time in the countryside where the

animals could eat you! It made for interesting walks back to the boathouse in the evenings, as it was around half a mile from the main farm and pitch black at night. I would walk along with a torch in one hand and my camera in the other half hoping to see a bear and half praying I didn't. There were a lot of coyotes in the area and at night sound travel a long way, so their barking and howling made them sound as though they were just around the next corner.

On top of the farm being a wonderful place, Dirk had a kayak! I may have misled Dirk into thinking I knew how to kayak, as I hate people watching me learn how to do things. I would much rather just figure it out by myself privately.

So I got to take the kayak out into the ocean, this time with a life jacket! But yeah you guessed it, capsized right away but quickly realised I had tried to set off into the waves and there was a sheltered area around the next point. Attempt two and success. I was off and out playing on the ocean, wow, it was good! I played in the bay for a couple of hours that day finding my balance and learning how to best deal with the waves.

I took the kayak out twice more during my stay there, each time getting better and more skilled and confident. Once I figured that the waves were all about timing your strokes right, they were quite good fun. Sadly though I could only spend two weeks there as I needed to head to New York to meet some friends.

I returned to Canada about six weeks later via train from New York to Toronto. Wow trains in North America are in the dark ages!

I planned to make my way across Canada from Toronto to Vancouver, stopping off in the big cities along the way. Wow Canada is big! I was in Toronto and I needed to get to Calgary to see my mate from Scotland who lives there now. I put an ad up on the Craigslist rideshare site and connected with a guy going my way, he just needed to sort out car insurance which he was doing. So I checked out of the hostel I was staying at as the guy was going to pick me up at four o'clock. However at three after multiple attempts I got hold of him on the phone only to find out he had bailed on me.

The Toronto film festival was on and now the hostel was booked up along with everywhere else in Toronto. I didn't have many options and decided to take a leaf out of Mareike's book. (A German traveller girl I met in Halifax) and catch an overnight bus out of Toronto and hitchhike my way across the prairies to Calgary. Mareike, had done some hitchhiking in Nova Scotia so I figured if she could do it, so could I. (Blood, muscle, skin and bone after all!) It was pouring rain as I was at the side of the road with my thumb out. I wasn't very hopeful but a camper van pulled in. It was an old retired couple who stopped because they didn't want anybody bad to pick me up. Next there came an old French man who couldn't speak English very well but insisted he was an English translator! The attempted conversation was highly amusing. Followed by an interesting character driving a bread delivery van who insisted on throwing tobacco out the window each time we passed a dead animal on the road to help the spirit pass on to the afterlife. He also told me he was on the run from the cops...

Then came three young girls who had been out partying the night before, and were looking a bit worse for wear. They thought it would be fun to pick up a hitchhiker. They dropped me off at a remote spot north west of Sault Ste Marie. It was getting dark but there were two hotel signs so I thought I would be all right.

After hiking up the road a couple of hundred meters it became obvious that the hotels were derelict and I realised I could be in a spot of bother. Lucky for me a guy stopped and gave me a lift all the way to Winnipeg. He had hitchhiked this road in the '70s and said he got stuck at the same area for a week!

I stopped off in Winnipeg for a few days as the hostel I stayed in was run and owned by an interesting guy who wrote a book called "The True Intrepid" a story about a world war two spy from Winnipeg who was Ian Fleming's inspiration for James Bond. It's quite hard to believe James bond is from Winnipeg, But he is and it's a great story of how this spy created a false background so no one could trace his true origins.

From Winnipeg I found a ride share with a girl named Rayna to Calgary. She had just returned from five years touring Europe with her wee dog which she had a passport for too. She hadn't driven for a long time, so I ended up doing a lot of the driving. I spent some time in Calgary staying with Gordon, my mate from Scotland. When I was in Winnipeg it was autumn and starting to get cold so I had updated my travel wardrobe with warmer clothes, however Calgary was back to shorts and t-shirt weather.

The next rideshare I organised fell through at the last minute too, so again I jumped onto the Greyhound bus but this time all the way to Vancouver.
There I met up with Matt whom I had met traveling around Asia the year before. But hanging around Vancouver was a sure way to spend all your money, so it was back to the
wwoofing. I found myself on a wwoof site on the Sunshine Coast north of Vancouver. It wasn't as good as Annie and Dirk's as the people who were there had had a busy summer and now it was time to relax, which meant smoking a lot of marijuana. I didn't fit in well. Luckily there were plenty of opportunities for adventure. The wwoof site was a camp ground in Egmont near the Skookumchuck Narrows, where there is an incredible standing wave that is generated when a three-meter high tide changes and pushes 200 billion gallons of water through a narrow channel. During the tide change there can be a two meter difference in the level of the water on either side of the narrows. White water kayakers surf the standing wave, and sometimes seals and sea lions do too! However, the water looks very turbulent and there is a deadly undercurrent. I had been well warned you must be very experienced in order to kayak it safely.
I wanted to get someone to take me out and show me how to white water kayak but I couldn't find anybody willing to take the time. There were some sea kayaks available for our use
at the campground so I went out the first time with a French wwoofer Alexis. It was only a two hour trip, but if I thought the Atlantic was good, this was amazing! The water was crystal clear and as calm as a

lake. You could see so much marine life; seals were everywhere in the water and on the rocks soaking up the sun. I was paddling all over the place, loving the feeling of propelling the kayak in the water. It was rhythmic and soothing but you could feel it in the muscles and it felt good. I was well hooked!

A week or so later I decided to take the kayak out on a day trip somewhere. It would have to be a solo trip as I didn't think Alexis would be up for what I had planned. I searched Google Earth and found a beach at a place called Vancouver Bay up Jervis Inlet. It was 13 miles from Egmont, which meant a round trip of 26 miles (40k). I believed it was manageable if I got a good start. I decided that if I wasn't there by lunchtime I was going to turn around as I was not prepared for an overnight stay and this being my first journey, I really had no idea how long it would take me.

The Kayak was a fibreglass Nimbus and cut through the water like a hot knife through butter. The trip out was great. I was so excited to be out on my own, on the water alone with the wildlife. There were lots of seals bobbing about all the time and, as I kayaked, all of a sudden there was a great loud blow and snort behind me, only about 10 meters away, scared the crap out of me. It was a Sea lion surfacing and they seem huge when they're that close. He got as big a fright as I did and took off in a hurry. I carried on with my eyes and ears on high alert for more wildlife; every floating log in the water was a surfacing whale (until it didn't move). This was late October and the weather was fantastic I kayaked in t-shirt and shorts.

I arrived at the beach and there was a dock with a large old abandoned building. Sitting there on the dock eating my lunch was amazing: the water was crystal clear and very calm and you could see the reflection of the mountains in the water on the bright bluebird day. It felt like I was sitting in a postcard only there wasn't a soul in sight. I stopped there for about an hour to eat lunch and take a wee hike around the place. It was strange hiking through the woods by yourself. I was highly alert for the slightest movement or sound to indicate a bear was near. Although I really wanted to see the wildlife, there're is an obvious part of me that does not want to get eaten too, so the first thing I did was find a good clubbing stick before I hiked around. Time was running out and I didn't want to kayak in the dark so I started headed back, on the way home the water got a wee bit choppy and I was fighting the tide, so it was more difficult. And it was getting late, cold and starting to get dark but I made it back to Edgemont alright and thought I had done well for my first real trip. I was as giddy as a child getting their first bike. The means and the freedom to explore set my imagination alight with wilderness possibilities.

My next outing was a trip to Harmony Falls at Freil Creek, around the same distance as Vancouver Bay. This time I set off a bit earlier to give myself more time to explore. It was foggy and I had to cross some water with the ferries lurking about, but I picked my moment and made it across the channel without incident.

Navigation was no bother: I had been studying Google Earth all week and knew the area well and there were plenty of geographical features. It seems easy when you know what shape the coastline should look like.

I saw plenty more Sea lions but this time they were further off so I just watched them for a while. They're fast in the water when they're going somewhere. I saw many eagles but every time I got my camera out they were gone!

The falls were not as impressive as I'd hoped as there hadn't been much rain that summer. I was hoping to have a good look around but it was not possible; there was nowhere to land, only big rocks on a steep slope. The kayak was fibreglass I didn't want to damage it trying to get in and out on the rocks. Still the trip was a good one, no exploring but I did get to paddle through several small islands, which is like exploring as you never know what's around the next corner. I was loving the ocean and really enjoying putting some effort into getting to places. It's a great feeling being alone in the ocean wilderness, enjoying the calm serenity of the places, but not really knowing what else you might see.

About a week later some locals were going out on a boat trip to collect driftwood from a beach to make into furniture and I managed to tag along. They took me out the Agamemnon Channel and around Nelson Island to Cape Cockburn with a driftwood beach; it really was a driftwood beach, It was covered in all sizes of wood. There was a cabin just off the beach; Sunray cottage was a log home built by a charismatic entrepreneur called Harry Roberts in 1929. Roberts is credited with naming The Sunshine Coast. The cabin is looked after by some locals for anyone passing by to use and enjoy. Just like me!

This was obviously going to be my next kayak trip, and what a trip it was going to be! It was going to be a 40 mile (65k) round trip so I would kayak out, spend a few nights in the cottage and kayak back. I planned the trip for the Halloween weekend. Everybody in the campground had been at a party so it was quiet the next morning. Apart from waking up Sweepy (a German wwoofer) to give me a lift with my stuff to the kayak I don't think anybody realised I was gone. This suited me just fine (as I didn't want someone to nag me about maps, radios, experience, groups etc.) However, I did tell Sweepy if I wasn't back in four days I might be it trouble! The trip out was the best yet! I went around the north side of Nelson Island and the bays were incredible! The ocean was alive with all kinds of creatures, all the different colours and shapes and sizes of the starfish amazed me! And the fancy houses dotted around the sheltered islands were impressive; it reminded me of a film I watched as a kid, "On Golden Pond." I loved that film about a city boy and an old man fishing on a remote lake. I was in heaven and counting my lucky stars that I had landed here, and was able to explore all this! The purple starfish were everywhere all clustered together. I was convinced it was their breeding time and I was seeing something rare! I since found out it is breeding but it's not rare.

It was windier this time so progress was a little slower, but the weaving in and out of islands was special. As I got around the west side of the island the waves were getting big! All of a sudden I was outside of my comfort zone, but I was so close- just around the corner and I'd be at Harry's cabin. I attempted to get around the cape but the waves were getting bigger and bigger. I was heading right into them, and when the kayak was seeing air at the crest and slamming down into the troughs of the waves I decided I was going to have to turn around! Now here was a problem! If I got caught sideways by one of these big waves I was going to capsize and would very quickly be smashed onto the rocks. An about face would have to be well timed and as fast as possible! I waited until I was at the top of the biggest wave and started turning away from the rocks, got the kayak around just as the next wave came and I was off like a rocket carried by the waves! Doing more steering with the paddle than paddling, I pulled into a nearby bay with a power station. There was no beach but there was a big tree in the water so I tied onto it and clambered up the banking. I was surprised at how tired and hungry I was. Paddling into the wind really takes it out of you.

I unloaded and hiked up to the power station. It was an unmanned booster station before the cables headed across the water, and high up so I could see the beach. I figured I could follow an old track down to Sunray Cottage. But I would have to leave the kayak there so I pulled it up the banking as high as I could and tied it off. I made it to the cottage in about an hour and got a fire started in the fireplace for some cooking. Boy was I hungry. I got cooking, well if you can call a big bowl of baked beans cooking! Food had never tasted so good. That night the wind and rain was howling! No window panes in the cottage so the wind went right through and the old place made a lot of noise. There was an old orchard behind the hut so I thought there might be bears around, but I figured since I was on an island there wouldn't be big ones, or cougars.

The storm lasted until the afternoon the next day and I was not kitted out for it, so exploring the area was limited to fetching firewood. I met a local couple out walking their dog on the beach and they told me some of the history of the hut and that there were in fact a lot of bears and there had been a sighting of a 9-foot cougar on the island!! Hmmm....

I knew bears could swim but I figured they would stick to the mainland as there would be a bigger foraging area, but cougars: I hadn't even contemplated them swimming. I had a fishing rod with me and had planned on catching some salmon, but I was having no luck off the beach with my limited lures. The locals I had met said there was a sheltered bay where they lived if I followed the old track, so I grabbed my rod and headed into the woods hoping the fishing would be better there. As I walked along the path I was very surprised to come across an area full of rubbish; it was scattered around everywhere. Further along there were a lot of old work vehicles left to rot. I figured it must have been the workers who built the power station that were to blame.

I had heard from a scuba diver that in the old days in Canada people would wait till deep into winter and then transport all their rubbish onto the middle of the frozen lakes and when the lake melted in the spring, Shazzam! Gone! (Guess there were no lakes about to get rid of the rubbish.)

He knew this as people now dive down and collect the old bottles and rubbish for souvenirs.

In the bay I was sheltered from the wind but was

still not having any luck with the rod. I thought this would be easy! After a good couple of hours I gave up and headed back to go exploring. There was not a lot to see and I soon got bored so I went back to try my hand at fishing once again. This time I was successful, I caught a fish but it was no salmon! It was a big ugly spiky thing; and I wasn't sure what it was. I hadn't thought of looking into which species I could catch apart from salmon! As I was unsure whether this species was edible, and since it was so ugly, I chucked it back! There would be no fish dinner for me that night. I later found out this fish was a rock fish and tasted like cod, bugger. The weather got a wee bit better that night but I had planned on catching salmon and didn't bring enough food to last the duration, so I decided to head back the next morning. I considered kayaking around the west then south side of the Island but decided not to as it would leave me exposed should the weather get bad again. I didn't do any sightseeing this time on the way back and the weather was not very nice. It was hard work and my shoulders were feeling it; they had not recovered from my trip out. I was exhausted by the time I got back to Egmont and as I had expected, no one realised I had been gone. I really enjoyed my days on the kayak but winter was closing in and I had my heart set on a winter in the Rockies for a bit of snowboarding. I set off and looked for a wwoof site in the mountains. After a disasters week in the Okanagan near Oliver on a wwoof site. I landed just outside Golden in the Blaeberry area to helping a couple (Pat and Elliot) with some renovations and right smack in the middle of a winter wonderland.

I had been involved in an incident on a wwoof site in the Okanagan which resulted in wwoof Canada treating me very unfairly. In light of the mismanagement of the situation by wwoof Canada all my previous wwoof hosts left the organization in disgust.

Despite the support from all my friends and hosts I had met through wwoof, the incident had left a very sour taste in my mouth. I had met a man named Pete in Dunster BC who helped me out a lot during the affair trying to set things straight, but after getting nowhere with wwoof.ca he recommended I move on and forget about it.

Planning my next adventure became the healthy distraction I needed! A snowboarding video set in Alaska rekindled my desire to visit the place. The only problem was getting there! My funds were running low! After some YouTube browsing I stumbled on a video of a group kayaking up the inside passage to Alaska. I thought "wouldn't that be a trip", but there was no way I would want to do it with a group. I wanted to do it on my own with the ocean and wilderness- it would be just like my fond memories of the Sunshine Coast paddling in a t-shirt in the gorgeous sunshine. I've had lots of crazy ideas and dreams and they never work out. So this was a dream that I didn't think would actually happen, but researching the logistics kept me occupied.

While I was going through the motions of researching the trip I had two friends from back home come visit me for some snowboarding. I had not seen Alec and Alun for about a year and snowboarding with them for those 10 days were fantastic. There's nothing like shredding a mountain with your mates! I noticed that travelling in Canada had changed me a wee bit. The guys were on holiday and the beer was flowing, but drinking had taken a back step for me and I wasn't missing it. My funds were also very low. When I told Al and Alec about my planned trip, they laughed and said they would see me back home soon. They both know me well and had heard a few crazy ideas come out of me in the years! Before Alec and Al came to visit I hadn't been sure if I'd wanted to keep travelling or re-join the rat race, but their visit hardened me, and I now knew that I wasn't ready to go back.

So I looked at ways to stay and the only possibility was to find some income as I was too old to get a work visa and even if I weren't I would have to go home and apply from there which I knew would be the end of the dream.

The only way I would be able to fund my Alaska trip was to find a source of income that didn't require a working visa. I searched Craigslist but I was in Golden at the time, and I needed to get to Calgary to have any chance of finding work. Once again I went to stay with Gordon who let me kip on his couch while I looked for work; I went down to the famous cash corner but no luck. After a few days I found some work outside Calgary shovelling gravel to build a retaining wall on a frozen lake. It was in the middle of nowhere and I didn't have any means of transportation. I knew I would need camping gear for the kayak trip and figured I could camp at the lake while I worked there. Purchasing the camping gear meant using the last of my money, i.e. my flight money home. This meant I was fully committed now: it was all or nothing. I was taking a big risk but it could prove to be the trip of a lifetime and I was game. The work was hard, shovelling all day, but I needed it to get fit for the trip so it was good and I pushed myself hard. Camping was a great way to test out the equipment even though it was -13 Celsius some nights. There were a lot of coyotes and wild dogs about but I soon got used to the howls but I didn't get used to the trains hooting in the middle of the night! It amazes me how big Canada is but how poor the train passenger service is; arguably worse than a third world country!

Gordon really helped by picking me up on the weekends and it was funny how things were starting to work out. I was surprised by the encouragement I was receiving in response to the trip- people kept telling me I could do it! I was beginning to believe I really could do it and there was the added incentive of not wanting to be another guy with big dreams but never doing anything about them. I got four weeks work in Calgary and then looked at getting to Vancouver.

I managed to find a rideshare that was to be the most interesting yet. I was picked up by this girl who started making drug deals on the phone within 5 minutes. She was a hallucinogenic dealer and started listing off all the crazy drugs she stocked. She told me she had been in the 6th dimension (but only for a few seconds)
and it was her goal in life to get across there permanently, (I have not seen her since so think she must have made it.) She picked up every hitchhiker on the way and would not pass anybody by who needed help and as a result, the car was packed for the majority of the trip to Vancouver.

I met up with Matt again in Vancouver and stayed with him as I set about looking for a kayak and gear. It was proving more costly than I had expected and I realised I needed to find more work. I did manage to buy an old Current Designs Storm kayak for 750 dollars, delivered. I think I got the kayak at a bargain because it had faded from red to an unsightly pink colour in the sun. But a deal is a deal! I found work relatively easy but it was on the other side of the city, I had made some friends in Vancouver through my travels and a friend of a friend lived close to the job site. Lisa was kind enough to let me stay at her place while I worked and indulged me in my wacky idea, but she was sceptical about whether I would make it in one piece! Lisa did say on more than one occasion that she thought I ought to take a spot GPS device and radio, but this was something I would not budge on. I had seen a documentary a few years back "Alone in the wild" about a Scotsman who went to live in the Canadian wilderness for three months. He only lasted seven weeks and was in a right sorry state by the end and had to be rescued. I believe when you don't have the option of calling for help you make the right decisions; you're more careful, and you spend your time dealing with your problems and sorting them out, instead of
thinking about pressing the call for help button. I also wanted to experience the true wild where you needed your wits to get you out of trouble and not a big bloody helicopter! That's what really appealed to me the most. There is also that song by a British group Pulp
"You want to live like common People:"
But still you will never get it right,

'Cos when you're laid in bed at night,
Watching roaches climb the wall,
If you called your dad he could stop it all,
You'll never live like common people.

I knew I would never live like "Grizzly Adams" if I could stop it all with the touch of a button! However, without a radio or GPS transmitter, I was faced with the problem of finding a way to let people know I'm still alive. I knew my mum would worry and I'm sure a few of my friends would too. I could phone in when I found a phone but that seemed a bit flaky as it was going to be remote. I came up with the idea of starting a blog and asking people to write in when they saw me. I was sure I would meet people on boats and they would be able to follow my progress themselves if they wanted, so I called it "spotthescot.wordpress.com," got some letter stickers, and plastered it onto the side of the kayak. Next on the list of equipment I would need were maps, and they were expensive. It was going to cost me $120 to get the proper ones. I decided I would just print off Google Maps of the areas I would be in. I had been planning my route for a month and knew the maps quite well, so I just zoomed in on the bits I needed. I ended up with around 25 sheets of A4 in two Ziploc bags. There wasn't a lot of detail on the maps, but from past kayaking experience I knew if I had the general layout of the coast I would be fine. My brother Malky said I would need a good compass but I didn't think it would do me much good. I did find a wee ball compass on a key chain for two dollars and thought that should do the trick but just in case I splashed out and bought two!

My mate Matt had encouraged me to video the trip and I thought it was a good idea so that was the next biggest expense. I got a Contour GPS camera which sounds great! However, it didn't have a display screen, and you could only access the footage and GPS data through a computer with an Internet connection so I wouldn't be able to see what I had filmed until I was back in civilization. However, it was small and didn't consume much power.

I looked high and low for something to charge the camera but the solar devices available were expensive and didn't look like they could take punishment from salt water. I found a windup torch with a USB connection for $16. It was meant for a quick phone charge but I thought it would do the trick. Next I had to get some proper fishing equipment and after forking out $250 for that, I was rather worryingly only left with $290 to my name. That was it, everything I had. I planned on fishing for my meals, but also I took lots of rice and pasta as well as the ingredients needed to make sauces and some potato mash to round out my diet. If the worse came there was also seaweed! I had looked into its edibility and had found that it's full of vitamins but hard for the stomach to take too much of.

Chapter Two
The Power of One

Finally I was all ready to set off. One week after
the 2011 Stanley Cup riots in Vancouver, Lisa gave
me a lift down to Kitsilano Beach. She had to zip of
to work so I was left to start my journey on my own.
The sun was shining and I persuaded a guy out
walking his dog to take a picture of me with the
kayak. I told him what I was planning to do and he
asked "does the press know about this? "Ha-ha, no!
What a feeling it was jumping into the kayak and
taking those first strokes on my journey to Alaska!
No matter what happened now, the planets had
aligned and through what seemed like amazing
strokes of sheer luck I had made it into the water. At
the start of this dream if I had taken the "safe" path
there is no way this would have happened. I have
learnt that sometimes if you gave it your all and are
willing to fly by the seat of your pants, sometimes
dreams can come true. (I'm sure that sometimes they
don't but how else will you know?) The whole time
this plan had been hatching in my head I knew that
the hardest part was going to be getting into the kayak
and on my way. Physically I knew my muscles would
adapt well to kayaking every day, but my body had a
habit of stopping my dreams. My shoulder has
dislocated since I was 17 and has been a spanner in

the works ever since. But it had taught me how to handle pain as it's unlike many other injuries. Normally when you hurt yourself only time and painkillers will help, but a dislocation is different; if you can get it back in, there is instant relief. The best way I found to get it back in was to simply relax through the pain and pull it back in. Feels funny and makes some crunchy noises, but it works. Mentally I was confident; when things get tough I am usually able to laugh at the situation or laughing at getting myself into said situation! I figured I was going to need to see the funny side of things a loton this trip.

I kayaked through the big cargo ships in Burrard Inlet and was heading to Bowen Island. It was a beautiful morning and I made good time, getting to a lovely beach on Bowen in time for lunch. What a great first stop! There was a grand view of the Vancouver metropolis, but from the wilderness! It was so lovely that I wanted to stop and set up camp for the night but thought I could make it to the north side of the island before the day was out. Mother Nature had other ideas however!

After packing up my lunch things, I headed out of the small bay and around the west side of the island where I encountered the wind. I fought it for two hours getting nowhere and finally pulled into a wee beach to see if I could sit it out for an hour. After an hour the wind hadn't died down at all but the beach I was on had a couple of houses and I didn't want to camp there in case the residents objected. I tried again to get around the west side but eventually ended up giving in and heading right back to where I had my lunch. It didn't take long to get there with the wind on my back, and the bay was nicely sheltered. I set up camp and got my fishing rod out. I put on a flashy spoon and spent around an hour fishing the bay when BANG! – I got one! I was high up on the rocks and had to pull it around to the beach to land it what turned out to be roughly 5lb. I was so happy and very excited as I took it back to camp. While I was cleaning the fish at the shore a dog walker approached and said "well done, did you catch that here?" Catching a salmon on the first try was exciting, and meant a lot to me as I was going to need this. My Scottish accent comes out very strong when I'm excited and I blew him away with a torrent of words he obviously didn't catch; he just laughed and said "you're Scottish then"

He told me it was unusual to catch salmon off the rocks like that and was impressed. I asked him which kind of salmon it was, as they all look the same to me. He thought it was a small spring salmon (Chinook).

He left me to figure out how to cook it up which I was glad of, as I had never cooked a fish I had caught. I decided to cook it the way I had seen Ray Mears cook his (Ray Mears is a British survival expert) Mears' method involves gutting it, cutting the head and tail off, and prying the bones out with your fingers along the spine and down the ribs. Then, using a split stick and two thin sticks to spread it out and prop it up in front of an open fire. It tasted very good but I think I wasted a lot of meat with my bad technique.

The light was dying and it was time for bed at the end of day one. As I was settling down into my sleeping bag, a boat tugging a barge full of trees/drift wood logs pulled into the bay. I thought they were just going to anchor in the safety of the bay for the night as it was already dark but they manoeuvred the barge near the beach and proceeded to unload the trees by pushing and pulling with a mini digger on the barge. It took them two hours! It was very noisy, but eventually they finished and I got some peace and quiet and was soon off to sleep. Waking up in a hammock on the beach next to the ocean waves makes you feel alive, and when I say next to the waves I mean 10 feet away! So there was a spring in my step as I packing up my camp. In no time at all I was on the water and on my way.

A wee bit of drizzly rain and a choppy sea, but I made it around the island and onto the Sunshine Coast easy with a little wind on my back this time.

I stopped off for a late breakfast on a long pebbly beach on the mainland and then headed up the coast. I made good time and stopped at Henderson Beach, Roberts Creek for a stretch as my back was killing me. A man came down to the beach to throw back some undersized Dungeness crabs. He was Harry from Newfoundland and I quizzed him about catching and cooking them, I had bought a cheap foldable crab trap and had watched YouTube videos on how to cook them but I find it never hurts to ask! Cleaning the crabs seemed a bit gruesome but I was going to have a problem with boiling them as I only had a small pot. He was interested in my trip so this was my first opportunity to pimp my blog and I gave him the details hoping he could put a wee message up and my mum would see I'm alive. Harry convinced me to try and cross over land into Sechelt Inlet. The town of Sechelt (which is a First Nations word meaning "land between two waters") is a narrow strip of land stopping the Sunshine Coast from being an island. I took his advice, and off I went.

It was easy getting there with the afternoon wind on my back. I parked up on the beach at Sechelt and started looking for ways to get over. The land crossing was a bit further than I had anticipated. The kayak was fully loaded and I would have to ferry all the stuff across in about three loads, which wasn't going to work unless I got someone to watch my things at each end. You can get wheels for a kayak that strap on and you pull it like a big suitcase. So I thought if I could find a kayak shop I could borrow a pair. The beach was busy but I asked a girl reading a book to watch my stuff while I looked for a shop. Found one called Marine and Mountain Adventure Outfitters shop and popped my head in.

Explained my situation to the woman and she got the owner and he loved my story! He ended up collecting my kayak in his truck and transporting me to Porpoise Bay Provincial Park. He said I could camp there and set off in the morning and threw me two boil in the bag readymade meals. He also told me he heard a rumour that there was a sighting of a 15-foot shark in the Inlet!

I knew Great Whites had been spotted on the B.C. coast before but would I be that lucky?? (Or unlucky!)

I was feeling very lucky! There was a campsite but I chose to camp at the water with my kayak. Didn't think I would get in trouble as my hammock blended in well and you could hardly see me. I didn't waste any time in tucking into the readymade meals. They were priced $10 each, they should be good! Yuck, they made my cooking seem like Gordon Ramsey's finest dish and they were $10 a pop.

Later in the evening I was sitting at a bench reading a book called Edible plants of B.C. I thought it might come in handy. When a vehicle stopped and a girl got out heading straight for me. I thought I was going to get asked to leave. But she asked if I was the guy kayaking to Alaska. I was a bit surprised until she told me she had been in the kayak shop and they had told her about me, and felt she needed to meet me. She was a native princess who looked like she could have been from Scotland; she was short with long dark ginger hair. She also enjoyed kayaking. I talked to her for quite a bit. She told me how this was a spirit quest of mine and it was going to change the world! She also mentioned she was really into her crystals, and was going to coordinate a crystal chime with others around the world, and she was excited to see what was going to happen. Something big I think she believed. She was a very interesting character and truly had a heart of gold. She gave me some advice about my trip. To ask permission to land if I came across a native settlement was to hold my paddle up over my head with both hands; if I was ever scared of the water I was to put both hands in the water and ask for safe passage; confronted with a bear I should talk to it and reason with it. After all this I was thinking she might be a bit flaky. Until she asked me about my trip so far as she felt there was a reason we found each other. So I told her all about my trip so far and mentioned that the hardest thing was a sore back from the kayak seat. At which point she went to her car and produced an inflatable backrest for kayaks. Ha-ha, who was I to doubt all this! I was amazed!

She also said she felt since I was so far from home I didn't get a proper send off for my spirit quest and she was here for that also. So she gave me a toonie ($2 coin) for me to give to a native chief up in Alaska and a small crystal rock to keep me safe with some advice on greeting Natives. This was all good advice and producing the backrest made me not doubt a word she said. The planets were still aligned!!

Up and away the next day with thoughts of great encounters with sharks. It was overcast and there was a band of mist high up in the mountains and a calm ocean, which made for a great kayaking. This was getting into the real wild. There were no more houses or roads, just ocean, mountains, trees and the only thing breaking the silence was my paddle strokes. The sun broke out into a gorgeous morning and there is no place like the Sechelt Inlet on a good day. It was simply, truly beautiful. I didn't go far when I found a beach where I just had to spend the rest of the day and night, Halfway Beach opposite Salmon Arm Inlet. I spent the day

fishing and sorting out my gear. Just caught rock fish and used one for bait for the crab trap. Harry had said to leave it in for a couple of hours. But I forgot about it and five hours later pulled up some starfish and sea cucumbers. Threw them back and began to doubt my tackle, although it was a great area. All through the night there was a sound of a generator, most annoying. I packed up the next day and was off. This was the start of leaving gear behind by mistake. I had tied my food up and slung it up a tree to stop the bears getting it. This method of

putting your food in a safe zone to protect it from bears made me wonder what happens when the bears are attracted by the smell of food but can't get to it? Do they go for the next best thing like you? Didn't forget the food but forgot to pack
away the rope!

Fitting everything into the kayak is no easy feat! Everything has to go a certain way and you have to take your time and do it properly. I have the patience of a five year old, so this is a real task for me. All my gear was packed into the kayak and a lot of it tied down on the top in waterproof bags and my camp tarp. I suppose I looked like the kayak version of a hobo with all his life belonging stuffed into a supermarket trolley!

I had thought of bringing my kilt with me on the trip as it goes everywhere with me. Some of my best travel tales involve the kilt, like the time in a Miami nightclub when the biggest meanest looking juggernaut of a man came straight across the dance floor with everybody scattering out his way right up to me
and points and says "you're the only people in the whole world who can make a skirt look hard" andthen walks off. And the time on a remote
Indonesian beach on New Year's day walking along the scorching sand and a big line of locals sitting on a wall all laughing until the last one stands up and shouts "Braveheart Freedom!!"
I had envisioned standing on a cliff with my kilt on and a cruise ship going past with all the passengers going, "Hey Captain, I think we are off course!" I'm sure it would make the news. But sadly there was no room for my treasured world companion.

The source of the noise during the night was a fish farm around the corner. They couldn't pick a nicer place for one! Today I was going to pass through the Skookumchuck Narrows and as it was way too fast, I was going to wait till the change of the tide (slack tide) when the water is not gushing through. But I timed it all wrong and ended up having to wait for five hours. But I was able to wait at the viewing point so there were lots of people there and I met a few and passed on my tale and blog.

Got through and headed to Egmont where I had stayed the year before. Was expecting to see the people who were there last time but they had moved on. I was looking forward to them telling me I was totally crazy. I decided to head to the restaurant there for one of their famous burgers. It was good and the waiter had been at the narrows that morning and left his baton which I had found, so I returned it to him and he explained what it was for, which I found most amusing, It was a police extendable

baton and he said it was for the bears. Apparently if you whack a bear in the groin with one of these the bear will run away, I didn't like to argue that if you were close enough to whack a bear in the balls you would probably be missing a head but oh well each to their own.

Up early and looked for a way to get online to check the blog but there was nowhere open. I was sure people had updated my blog for me as enough people said they would.

I headed off and followed the route I did to Sunray cottage the year before. In the distance I could see Harmony Falls and they were gushing out of the trees

in a roaring spout and thundering down, I could
clearly hear them and they were about 6 miles (10k)
away. Would have been nice to go and see but it was
out my way and Alaska was calling me.

As I was passing an island I noticed movement and
immediately turned the kayak in that direction. There
was a foe deer on the rocks below the forest and it
was looking at me, so

I kept still and glided in. I was around 100 feet
away but if I made a move, like to go for my
camera, it would be off so I decided to just enjoy
this moment for myself. As I got close I noticed the
mother just inside the forest looking at me as well
trying to figure out if I was a log. When I got 50 feet
close the mother decided I wasn't a log and stamped
her feet and the foe scrambled up the rocks and they
disappeared into the woods. Now I'm a big meat eater
and I could kill a deer for food if I had too, but I
would get no pleasure out of it and don't understand
how anybody could. These personal moments with
nature felt really good and it was extra special
because it was just me, my very private moment and
nobody around to say don't be daft it's just a deer.
The wind came up in the early afternoon and I took
shelter in Vangard Bay, The rocky beach was covered
in oysters. So I cooked some up. I just put about an
inch of water in a pan and the oysters, and covered
the pot until they popped open. This was the way I
was shown to cook quahogs in Nova Scotia the year
before and I figured it would work for oysters. I made
up a creamy garlic cheese sauce to have with them.
This was my first time having oysters and I was a
little unsure but they're just like big mussels and I
munched them all down. Moved on into the wind but

it was tough. Got to Hardy Island and tried some more fishing with no
luck, but lucky for me there were more oysters. The rules for camping in the wild with bears about say you should camp well away from cooking areas and store your food up a tree and well away, but this does not work out well with me. My kayak would have smelled of food and there wasn't anywhere to go, plus I was always hungry so trekking off to eat seemed ridiculous. So I altered things slightly. I stored my food in the kayak for easy getaway in the morning, and I would dampen a rag with a bit of stove fuel and put it on a branch next to the kayak. I figured that the smell of the fuel would mask the food smell. I would start a small fire at night and let it smoulder through the night to keep animals away. There was no danger of forest fires with all the rain, the main reason I opted for a
Hennessey hammock was I would be off the ground and high up. Animals all fear bigger animals and do not like looking up so I figured this was a lot better than lying on the ground like a hotdog in a tent. Plus I knew there would be a lot more camping areas open to me as I didn't need level ground. Next day I crossed back onto the mainland up past Powell River. At the pulp mill there is a breakwater made with old concrete ships from World War II. Amazing you can make concrete Ships, and they're still afloat. This whole section of coast was packed with unwelcome looking houses with private signs up all along the beaches, not what I was expecting. I longed for feeling more remote and away from rules and regulations, well, people really. I had a long day and was desperate for a stop but there was nowhere good.

So I parked up on this rocky beach but after I unloaded and had a walk around for a water source I found a sewage outflow, not nice!

I took a walk inland through the woods looking for a better source and stumbled on an area full of salmon berries so I was helping myself as I went, until I heard something big moving in the bushes. It was a bear munching on the berries, he was not aware of me so I talked to him but he didn't seem to notice. He was obviously in a world of his own and just kept munching away until I clapped my hands and gave him a shout. He crapped his pants and took off like Usain Bolt through the bushes. Well that's the first bear encounter out of the way I thought.

I couldn't find a good water source I was happy with. I didn't trust my water filter to make clean water from potential pollution from built up areas and I had no idea what was in the area. I just knew there were towns on both sides of me not far away. So I just headed back and made do with what I had. I slept with one eye open that night since I was so close to the berries and I was sure a bear would come by and check me out.

Set off the next day and I hadn't travelled far when I noticed an otter perched on a rock eating a fish. I got up close and watched him eat, he didn't seem to mind me watching but he did keep an eye on me. After he finished his gourmet sushi he slid into the water and it was now his turn to check me out. He swam around me and then followed me for 10 minutes. He was very inquisitive, just like me, but I must have bored him eventually or he got hungry again. Further up there was a boat in the water leaning at an odd angle,

the closer I got it appeared that it had run aground.
There were big rocks or I should say monoliths
sticking up out the water all over the place. The tide
was out and it was early
morning. It looked like the captain had tried to take a
short cut around the warning buoys or it was dark and
he didn't see them.

The coast guard was there overseeing things so I took
the opportunity to park up and have breakfast. It was
like a live episode of "Deadliest Catch." The crew
was sitting on the high side of the boat with the coast
guard circling around looking for damage. But
nothing exciting happened. The coast guard just
waited in the area in case the situation got worse.
Looked like they were waiting for the tide to come in
to try and get free. It must be one of the most
embarrassing things for a captain of a fishing boat.

A couple of years before this I was working in
Singapore and enjoying a few beers with some Irish
work colleagues when we bumped into the captain of
the first Irish sponsored boat to take part in an around
the world sailing competition. Although he had no
boat, as he had wrecked it on rocks, sinking it, and he
and crew needed rescue by other boats in the
competition. He was a very embarrassed,
disappointed, ashamed looking man but in true Celtic
style me and the guys never let up with the jokes all
night. Captain Nemo was told to sink his drink on
more than one occasion!

Anyway I thought I better get my ass moving if I
was going to make good distance today. Fishing
was not going well. I was trolling the lures the guy in
the shop told me to use but I was catching
nothing! This was worrying me a bit as I needed

the fresh food and it would save me a lot of money. I needed to cross over from the mainland to the Johnston Strait, which starts at Campbell River. I was going to island hop over and on my way there was an island with a beach full of oysters and they were a lot bigger than the others I had found.

Decided to stop for lunch and cooked them with a bit of camp made garlic butter. Mmmm, heaven!

As I made my way from the beach I realised I didn't have my watch in its usual place in my life jacket. Oh no. It had proved handy to have and I knew I would struggle without it. Time passes funny when you're in the middle of nowhere and it would be easy to overdo the kayaking without it so I turned back hoping to find it even though it was 30 minutes kayak. When I got back to the beach the tide had come in and I wasn't hopeful. After I retraced my steps I gave up. Then as I was kayaking out again I noticed it under the water. It must have fallen out when I was packing up to go. I just managed to reach it and trying to remember if it was waterproof as I just bought the cheapest one I could get before leaving for the trip. Turned out it was splash proof and that was good enough. Anyway off again; second time lucky. I made it to the southeast side of Cortes Island and made my way around the south side of the island looking for somewhere to camp as I was tired. Every time I saw an accessible good looking campsite there was a private property sign saying "no camping." I was getting very annoyed and frustrated. There were no houses, just woodland and beach, but lots of signs. I crossed my fingers I would be away from this madness soon. Then I got around to the west side and I noticed a guy and dog sitting on the rocks with an improvised shack just in the woods. I asked if it was okay to set up camp and he said it was Crown land and I could camp anywhere I liked. He looked like he liked his privacy and to be honest so did I so I picked a site further down. I think he must have been a bit of a hermit as his camp looked like it had been made up with junk. This was day seven, so my first whole week was in the bag. I had come around 120 miles (190k).

But my body was starting to hurt. For the past couple of days I was getting bad pins and needles in my forearms. Two years ago I worked too hard over the space of a week doing heavy lifting and long hours with no time to recover; we were working 18-20 hours a day. We had a short time to do the work as we were in a foreign country and needed to be out by a certain time, and I believe I damaged nerves in my left forearm. I was taking a holiday straight after the job and didn't want to cut it short so just drank more beer for the pain. Went to the doctor when I got back to Scotland but was told I would have to wait 16 weeks to see a specialist! So yeah, by the time that came around it felt fine and I was off on another job in Singapore.

Day eight and I was in trouble; left forearm was numb, throbbing with the pins and needles. I decided to take the day off as I needed supplies and well couldn't even tie my shoelaces. I decided the problem was holding the paddle too tight and that if I could change the position of my grip this might help. I had a pair of flip-flops with a Velcro strap instead of the toe column that keeps them on your feet. I had bought these flip-flops in Vancouver after dragging Lisa all over looking for ones with Velcro. She tried and tried to get me to buy the other ones but stubborn me refused as they hurt my feet. At the time I never knew how handy they would be. I tied the flop onto the paddle and Velcroed my wrist in so only my fingers would be gripping and not the palm of my hand. Hopefully this and a day off would sort things out.

Cortes Island was interesting! I had landed right smack in the middle of hippieville. Managed to find the town and get supplies in the local co-op.

They also had a burger stand and I could not help myself. I ordered the biggest cheeseburger they had and it was succulent juicy meaty

Heaven!

On the way back to my campsite there was a 4x4 pulling a trailer full of kayaks which stopped at a shop. So I asked them about crossing over to Campbell River and up the Johnston Strait. The girl said "you know about the water at Campbell River don't you? You know you have to get through at slack tide?"

"Em sure." I said. Luckily her friend came back and I got to escape before she started asking questions like "do you know what you're doing?" I knew the Strait was going to be fast water as a lot of water must pass through it as the tide changes and I thought I would make good time on it. But what was she on about? She seemed to talk about it as if there was a lot of danger to it. Anyway I decided I better take her advice and hit it at slack tide.

Up early to catch Campbell River at slack tide. I didn't bother with tide charts as I didn't know how to read them well enough. Plus they seemed daft to me when you're on the water and you can see it's going out and coming in you know it's going to change in 7-8 hours. I always camped high above the tide mark, too and well, I was in the trees with the hammock so no chance of floating away in a tent.

Got to the opening of the strait and oh dear! The water was strange! It was like the water was vibrating if you put a cup of tea on top of a washing machine on spin cycle you get a similar result, and strange waves would appear out of nowhere. There are speedboats, fishing boats, cruise ships, and ferries. There might have even been a few submarines, all in a narrow stretch of water. As I crossed over to the Campbell River side I noticed the coast guard in a speedboat with about six men in it stop near the bank and watch me. I just powered across as fast as could but I had to learn quick as I was encountering some crazy water. There were big whirlpools opening up in front of me and if I caught one it would try to spin the kayak. Then there were sink holes and when I put the paddle into one of these there would be very little resistance and it would off balance me!

So I had to react very quickly. Luckily I had taken off the flip-flop before crossing and just ignored the consequences of potential damage to my forearm.

After about five minutes the coast guard left me alone. Not sure if they thought I would be okay or if they thought just let the daft bugger drown and nominate him for a Darwin award! But I made it and felt I had passed a test and I was more confident in my kayaking. I just paddled right passed Campbell River as it felt better to camp in the woods and I would only end up spending money. I stopped for lunch just before Race Point.

Yep, you guessed it; it's called that because the water really races through there. I had to wait till slake tide the next morning to attempt it.

I had some time on my hands but there was a big kelp bed right in front of the beach so fishing seemed off the agenda. So I took a hike up the hill. The map said there was a road close, so thought I would have a look and maybe even pick up some local knowledge about the water. There was no path so I bushwhacked my way up, got to a driveway with big intimidating security gates and a sign saying guard dogs patrol this area. I was on the wrong side of the gates, inside the yard of a big house!

So I really did tiptoe my way back down to the beach. I was bored so decided to grab the fishing rod and go for a walk up the beach to hopefully find a spot to fish from. Just as I was getting to the corner I heard a big deep honk and loud music as if there was a disco party right around the corner! Then the biggest cruise ship I have ever seen came around the bend; it blotted out the landscape. It could barely fit in the narrow channel with high cliffs either side of it. I hoped I would not meet one of these giant monsters in a channel as narrow as this. It must be interesting moving on a boat as you are cruising by cliffs so close. I managed to climb around the cliffs and do a bit of fishing but it was useless as the water was moving too fast. However I was able to survey the area for the next morning, hitting it at slack tide was going to be essential. Good night's sleep but my forearm was still bad. I

was getting nervous as there was no way I could

make it to Alaska like this. Was my big trip going
to end this way? I had to find a way to fix this so I
could make it to Alaska. Maybe if I tried harder to use
it less and relax my grip more. I wasn't
confident this would work but I had to try.
So northward I headed, the channel was fast and I felt
safer on the edge but it was flowing the
opposite direction of the tide (backeddy). So there
was no let up. It was reactive paddling till it
opened out.
It was Canada Day and there were a lot of sport
fishermen out but I never saw anybody
catch fish. They did tell me that they had. I
however was having no luck! As I got up around
the corner of the channel I passed an RV/camp site
and just as I was debating whether they had a store or
not I noticed someone pulling up a flag on some
flagpoles they had near the dock. It was a Scottish
flag so I decided to investigate. I tied up to the dock
and went looking for the culprit, found him but soon
wished I hadn't. His great granddaddy was Scottish
and his first question was "what's your last name"
His next remark was classic "hell,
I'm more Scottish than you!" Haha. Was wondering
why I had stopped and two minutes later I was
looking for an escape route! But he was determined to
tell me all about Scotland, like how all the lakes are
not called lakes there called lochs.
 "Yes I know"
was my best reply to this. I had to bite my tongue as
my sarcasm was itching to come out, but I just asked
if there was a store. There was none, and none around
the area. His friend asked what I needed and I said I
could do with some flour, which they had plenty of.

This was very fortunate for me, maybe the reason he pulled that flag up just as I was passing was so I got some flour? Were the planets still aligned?

It was a wet miserable day and I was keen to get going to find a spot to set up camp. I continued up the Strait about four miles and found a good beach to stop and get the fishing rod out. Ten minutes later I had one! A rockfish but a good sized one. So I cooked it up, but didn't do a good job of it. My filleting skills were useless, I wasted a lot of meat but it was a good change and went well with the rice.

I made up some camp bannock for the next day; the bannock was just bread with raisins and pumpkin seeds in it. I baked it by putting it in my pan and on top of fire embers, turning it over regularly. I made it so I wouldn't need to stop for lunch the next day. Well that was the plan anyway. I ate half of it that night and half

in the morning. The channel had opened out a bit and the kayaking was a lot better but the weather was crap. I kayaked for about an hour and found a cool waterfall so decided to stop for some more breakfast and a boggle. As I was eating my cereal, two kayakers came along heading in the other direction. They were the first kayakers I had come across and they had all the gear: pristine kayaks with full dry suits on. I must have looked like a scruffy ill-equipped moron, and I asked where they had come from, and they said Port Hardy. I asked how far it was and how long would it take. Their reply was hard work, depends on how fast you kayak, the wind, tides. Okay I said how long if everything is average? Four days they reckoned. Then they started questioning me. When I told them I was heading to

Alaska they looked at each other and then my old kayak. They took a picture of me and then my kayak, talked to each other out of my ear shot, and then buggered off without even saying
bye!
I figured I wouldn't get a warm welcome from proper kayakers and didn't really blame them as my kit was substandard. So was my kayak; and if they knew my kayak experience! Well, better they didn't, but I suppose they guessed it. I was beginning to think I was out of my depth; the weather was nothing like the year before on the Sunshine Coast. I headed off and the weather was foul. I was feeling a bit low. My forearms were bad, my equipment was based on my kayaking experiences on the Sunshine Coast, and real kayakers obviously thought I was a joke. Maybe it was time to call it a day. What was I thinking!!
Later I was just plodding away when a fast boat went by and circled around the back of me. It approached from behind and I didn't know what to expect, when a girl came out onto the deck asking where I was off too. After I told her she said "we thought it would be something like that. We are a group of kayakers ourselves and we have a base camp up ahead on west Cracroft Island. We are on our way back to Vancouver but you should stop off. There are whales up ahead and we have a hot tub, and thought you might like these brownies!!" She handed me the brownies and sped off. Wow, could not have been timed any better. It was the perfect
pick me up. I scoffed the brownies there and then and headed on with renewed vigour and a big smile. So

not only were the planets aligned, they delivered brownies too!

The weather was not good and I didn't want to cross the channel to Cracroft Island in it, so stopped off for the day. That night I remembered reading about how some people slept with wrist guards on to help with carpal tunnel. So I slept with both my flip-flops on my hands as both my wrists were giving me bother now. Eureka! Next morning my forearms were much better. I had cracked it and the weather was fantastic. Nothing was going to stop me now.

I headed across to the northeast side of the channel as that was where Cracroft Island was. As I headed up, I was passing a bay and saw a shiny roof in the woods, so thought that would be the kayakers place. I went in to investigate. There was a big cabin. I parked up and shouted but there didn't seem to be anyone there and there were no kayaks about. Popped my head into the cabin and the sign said it was the Marks family home and people were welcome to come in make themselves at home and eat. You don't have to tell me twice.

I figured that this was the place the kayakers used but I didn't see their names in the logbook and it didn't look like anyone had been there in the past two days. I was convinced it was the right spot so I went on the look for the hot tub, however didn't find it. It was not the place the kayak girl had talked about. Oh well, I thought might as well make use of the cabin.

Decided to take the next day off, I had travelled over 200 miles (320k). Out on a walk that afternoon I noticed a bear foraging on the beach, turning all the stones over. I got my camera out and approached the bear. Now this might seem insane to most people, but as I was going to be living in these creatures' backyard for a long time, I needed to understand them better. I had talked to people and read a few books and there seemed to be two schools of thought:

First, they're all extremely dangerous and aggressive; second, they're very scared of humans and will not harm you so long as you don't get in between them and their cubs (different for grizzlies).

I believed the truth was somewhere in the middle: they were definitely dangerous, but must be scared of humans, as we kill them for sport and safety all the time.

I also decided that I would be safer in the wild than camping near civilisation. The bears would have time to get accustomed to man around towns, but in the wild we would be unknown and potentially very dangerous. So, when I had startled the bear in the berry field, it ran like hell. What would this bear do when he could see me approach? When I got close he stopped foraging and just looked up at me for about two minutes. I didn't move and it looked like he was checking me out to see if I was a threat, but then he just went back to seeing what was under all those rocks!

Back at the cabin I found a wee fishing book so thought I would school up and hopefully figure out how to be more successful. I dozed off for an afternoon nap. Ah, this is the life, but I was rudely awakened by a big animal at the side of the cabin. I thought the bear had come back and it was my own stupid fault, as I should have scared him off the beach by being more aggressive, now he wasn't scared. I banged on the side of the cabin but that didn't deter

him so I grabbed the big axe and charged out the door. Oops, it was not the wee bear from the beach. It was a much larger one!! But he must have been from the same Bolt family of bear as the bear in the berry bushes, and he took off like a bat out of hell.
So I learned that aggression was going to be my best defence if it came to it. Grizzlies were going to be a different story, but let's hope it wouldn't come to that!
I decide to make use of the big fire stove as they had it connected up to heat the water. I could have a hot shower, and I needed one! It had been nine days since my last one.
I cooked up some bannock on the big log stove, also with pumpkin seeds and raisins. It was a lot easier cooking it on a stove and I cooked four big buns. That evening I decided on a walk along the beach as the tide was well out. The walk was gorgeous and I found a big log to sit on and just watched the clouds going over the mountains at sunset.
Suddenly I had an amazing feeling that I can only describe as euphoria. It was like I was in the right place at the right time. Everything had led me to be here on this journey at this time, and everything was going to be all right. I don't know if it was the isolation or the physical exertion of the past two weeks. All I know was, the feeling was very real and I will never forget it.
The next day was overcast but I was hoping to make some good distance and maybe see whales! Not far and I noticed some people standing up on a hill to my right. It looked like a camp; more than likely the kayakers' camp. The people were watching something in the water. It was a school of dolphins or

porpoises! So I watched them too, and tried to video them with no real luck. I didn't go see the kayakers as they were not in the water and Alaska was calling and it seemed like I had been wasting time.

I powered away across the bay thinking the kayakers would be watching me and think wow he's fast! In reality they were probably thinking why's he taking so long!

There was a small island in the bay and just as I looked right an eagle dived into the water! It had caught a big fish but it was too big. The bird couldn't take off again and I was shocked to see what it was doing. It was doing the butterfly stroke to the shore! I never knew they could do that and couldn't take my eyes off. When he got to the shore he dragged it up and took a rest! Wow, I was well impressed: eagles could swim with a big salmon in their talons. You always see the wildlife documentaries with eagles swooping down and flying off with salmon, but never swimming with them, he was obviously knackered from the swim as he had his mouth open gulping in air, first time I had seen a bird short of breath too! There were a lot of porpoises and dolphins in the area so there was always something to watch. I was finally out of the narrow channel and it opened out to Queen Charlotte Strait. There's a lot of Islands to zip through and it was good. It was much better than kayaking in a never-ending channel of open water.

As I kayaked close to the islands I couldn't get rid of the idea of bears and cougars sitting on the branches waiting to pounce on me. Don't know where this idea came into my head but I was always looking for them.

I found a small island and decided to set up camp. Fishing still was not going well but the book in the Marks cabin said best thing to do was "keep trying." The island was full of big trees and there was not a lot of underbrush so I explored a bit. I came across trees with strips of bark cut at the bottom and pulled off, just about four inches wide to nothing at the top around eight feet. There were old ones and new ones so somebody came here to do this on a regular basis. I Had kayaked passed a few native wood carvings on the islands and thought it
had something to do with that, but could not think of what it would be. I later found out natives use it for making into clothes; it's called bark cloth. I would have never guessed. I thought it was maybe used in traditional canoes.

The next day it was really foggy so I slept in, hoping the fog would clear, but it didn't. I got bored and packed up; decided I could at least make it to the next big island. I could make some headway but I would have to stay close to the island and cross at the shortest gaps as the fog was really thick. It meant following the coastline right into the bays, since I couldn't see the other side. A compass would be no good because of the tide pushing you off course all the time, and no feature to head to. It was taking forever to get anywhere. Distance wise it was useless, but it was cold and kayaking was better than sitting about. I struggled that day but did make some headway.

The next day was the worst yet. The wind and rain was horrendous. I was breaking away from the protection of Vancouver Island, and fighting a northwest wind. I made about six miles (10k) that day and was beat; set up camp and hid in my hammock. I was thinking "what happened?" After kayaking in late October in a t-shirt and shorts last year, I thought my biggest problem on this trip would be overheating and I had been telling myself "it will get better" all the time.

Next day started out a lot better and I made some good distance. As the day progressed the wind picked up and so did the waves. Today I was trying to make it to Port Progress as it was on my Google maps. I was hoping to find a store there or maybe a restaurant with big juicy cheeseburgers. I battled the wind and waves and passing a fish farm and I asked one of the workers where Port Progress was. He didn't have a clue! There was no Port Progress but there was a safe anchorage for sail boats to take cover in bad weather. Bugger, I had run out of oats and they were an important part of my diet. They got me going in the morning. The place was called Ba'as or Blunden Harbour, Port Progress was a name given to it at the turn of the 20th century. It was a Native resettlement but it proved too hard to get to so it never lasted. Google maps is a little outdated and still has it as Port Progress.

There was a hut on the beach with a stove so I was happy with that. On a walk along the beach looking for a fresh water stream I came across a placard dedicated to a nine year old girl who had been taken by a Mountain lion (cougar) a year before. I had not really thought about cougars being a big problem on my trip as most people have never seen one, but now I instantly developed the eyes of an eagle and the ears of a bat, I was scanning the woods constantly.

There were about five sail boats tied up to buoys in the harbour and I had some visitors. Two women came by walking a dog; I got talking to them and asked how the weather was looking for the next few days. At that point one of them pulled out a radio and tuned it to the shipping weather channel, held it up to me and I listened to a bunch of gobbledygook. I think you must need to do a course to be able to understand that nonsense. But I just pretended to understand and said oh thanks, and when they wanted to show me something on my map I quickly changed the subject. I could just see their faces if I whipped out my printer paper Google maps! They told me there was still some remains of the wee town and the ruins were just up the beach, so I decided to investigate. The forest had reclaimed it all; just a few scraps of metal left over. The native settlement there had been relocated in 1964 to Port Hardy where it was not so isolated.

I also met an old guy who came to walk his dog. He told me everything changes around Cape Caution. There would be lots of whales and it would be a lot more remote. I was getting excited, but what was Cape Caution? It wasn't on my map...

I spent the evening baking bannock since I had the use of the stove and an early night, but the worst thing about staying in old huts and cabins is you are never alone, Usually you're the guest of the local mice population.

Next day I was off and it was a gorgeous sunny calm day. The view was incredible and I stopped off for lunch in the best place yet. It was a rocky beach with views of Vancouver Island in the distance. I tried to get pictures of me standing on the rocks there, but that's the problem with solo kayaking: nobody to take great pictures with me in them.

The area felt very remote and I felt I could have been the first person so sit on these rocks eating my lunch (bannock). That was part of the allure of this trip was to "go where no man has gone before" or at least feel like it! As I continued my quest north I noticed all the rocks seemed to be black. I had to have a closer look and it was mussels, bloody great big ones. I never knew they could grow that big. They were around 6-8 inches long and 4-5 inches wide.

Muscles are typically 2-3 inch long, so I was dumbstruck. To a hungry man this looked too good to be true. I was too cautious though as I had never seen them in restaurants before so maybe they were poisonous?. I set off wondering why they were so big in the area. Could it be that they all get this big if they're not picked or eaten?

Soon I heard a knocking sound coming from up ahead and saw a Sea otter floating on its back banging a shellfish on a rock on its belly. I have seen this on wildlife documentaries but it was great to witness it first-hand, although as soon as the camera came out, it dived. I'm sure animals can sense cameras. Soon there were Sea otters all around me banging away but all were just too far away for a good camera shot. It will just have to be locked away in the memory banks as another one of my very own special moment with the wild life. I guess they were eating the big mussels but they could have been eating oysters too. Maybe they would have been extra-large oysters also.

Anyway Alaska was whispering in my ear "Danny, Danny what's taking you so long, get your bloody ass in gear" As with every late afternoon for the past week the wind started to get up. As I just got around this point and there was a great big long sandy beach. I picked an area half way along the beach as there was a rock outcrop in front of it. As It was open to the full swell I thought this would protect me long enough to get into the water in the morning if the waves were big. I ended up having to battle an hour to get to it in the wind, but the beach was beautiful.

As I pulled the kayak up the beach and unloaded onto the beached logs I noticed something shiny in the woods. Upon investigation it was a mini hut, I had pulled up right in front of it! There was a logbook and a notice telling me it was a hut built by kayakers for kayakers. Well, the planets were indeed aligned. I felt like somewhere along the line Forest Gump's feather had landed in my kayak.

The beach was called Burnett Bay; the cabin has been there since 1985 and ever since people have been leaving notes scribbled on scrap paper and then notebooks started getting filled. It was great reading about all the different people using the hut, with their stories. Flicking through them I found people on the same trip as me years ago and they all seemed to be worried about Cape Caution, which I would encounter the next day.

I just hoped it would be a calm day but it looked like I would truly be exposed to the full swell for the first time as there's a big gap between Vancouver Island and Calvert Island.

The cabin was tiny just big enough for one or two, but it was cosy and there was a new stove in it, too. The only thing keeping me away from reading all the stories was the solitude and the amazing great beach all to myself. This was my first big sandy beach and I was being spoilt. It just shows you how remote the place was, when there was great sandy beach and nobody has built a bloody great big house on I, only had to kayak 18 days to get here. Each day it felt like my journey was just really beginning as I got more and more remote.

The next morning there were lots of dead dogfish washed up on the beach. There were around 50 of them. It seemed strange that they would all be washed up at the same spot, within about 30 feet. I took it they had been caught in a fishing net and had been thrown away as they didn't look that tasty.

I wanted to stay for a bit longer but the weather was good so I thought I better get this Cape Caution out of the way. It was a breeze. The weather was good and the full swell was not bad. It was just big rolling waves and the kayak just glided over them. But the power of the swell was obvious as it made contact with the rocky outcrops. The waves would smash into them and explode! Rather worryingly the swell also reviled hidden rocks just under the surface, I didn't want to get too close to the rocks then! There didn't seem to be anywhere to land around when it became time to camp hunt.

Although I could land on some of the beaches I doubted if I could take off the next day. I headed to an island and hoped I would find a decent landing on the north side, as the swell was coming from the southwest. On my way there I got my first brief whale sighting. I believe it was a Minke whale, going by the descriptions I have read and its behaviour. They are small for Whales and fast but it was far off and didn't entertain me by coming closer.

The island was really rocky and it looked like I was going to have a great time getting out and pulling the kayak up. As I came around the island I was really surprised to find a tiny beach totally sheltered from all sides in a wee bay. Eureka! It was perfect and I was amazed I had found it, plus there were some of
the big mussels on the rocks. After seeing the otters eating what I thought were probably the mussels, I decided to try them.

I steamed them and then fried them just to be sure, and it was like having mussel steaks, they were that big! I didn't have a lot just in case they were bad for you, but they were very tasty.

I was on Table Island, quite far off the mainland and with the swell there I decided it was highly unlikely there would be any bears. So that night I didn't see the need to start a fire and leave it smouldering all night. I went to bed that night feeling very safe and happy, it always felt better on an island. I enjoyed sleeping in the hammock, it felt a lot better being up of the ground and there was a gap between the mosquito net and the flysheet you could look out through. It gave great views of the surrounding area. One of the worst things I find about tents is hearing noises outside and having to stick your head out to get a better look.

As I slept, in the middle of the night I turned over and scared the hell out of a bear that must have been sniffing about just at the side of the hammock. I was

able to look out and just saw a big dark furry shape disappear into the woods, crashing and breaking every branch on the way. I was very surprised there were bears here and considered lighting a wee fire but I was too tired and after listening to all the noises for a bit, I decided it was long gone and I went back to sleep. Next day there were lots of very small deer prints on the beach and I figured
that must have been what had attracted the bear to the island. The island was way too small for
forging unless the bears went down at low tide for the big mussels. Now that would be a sight I would like to see!
I badly needed supplies as I had missed out Port Hardy thinking Port Progress would do, so I was going to have to make a detour and the most likely place seemed to be Duncanby Landing up Rivers Inlet. It was a bit out my way but I had no choice. So that's where I headed but I had not printed off a close up of the area as it was off my path so I had to do a lot of guessing. There were a lot of small speedboats out fishing so I followed where they were coming from and going to. They led me to Duncanby but as I approached it seemed like I would be lucky to find a store. I asked what
appeared to be locals if there was a store and they laughed and said, no, but there was a restaurant. I guessed the restaurant would be way too expensive for me so asked if there was a store near. They directed me to the only store around which was Dawsons Landing and it was 13 miles up the inlet, so off I went.
It was a long way as I had already
kayaked 18 miles (29k), but the wind was behind

me and I was able to use it and kind of surf some of the way. I had realised that I had not contacted anyone since I left Vancouver 20 days ago. I had hoped people had updated my blog, but there was no way of me knowing that. Everyone would probably be thinking I was dead.

Dawsons Landing is the only shop between Port Hardy and Bella Bella, a good four days kayak in each direction. It consisted of a bunch of floating platforms with a store and some cabins on them, with a few buildings on land that were owned by the fisheries department. The owner had a satellite phone and kindly let me use it to check in back in Vancouver. There was a bad connection but Lisa sounded really surprised and shocked. Oops, think she thought I had kicked the bucket. The connection failed but she phoned right back and it was a lot better. A couple of people had updated my blog, I was relieved to hear, and Lisa said she would check in for me on the blog and I would check in with her at Bella Bella, that had eased my mind a bit. After getting some much needed supplies: rice, oats, cereal, pasta, I met Larry there who was doing some work on the fisheries buildings. He told me about a big grizzly bear and a cougar in the area, both had been sighted within the past day. Also he told me a tale about a friend of his, He was standing on a beach looking out to sea, when a cougar came up behind him and mauled him. He did say the cougar was injured and starving which probably resulted in it attacking a grown man. His advice was never turn your back on the woods!

The owner of Dawsons said there was a place I

could camp further down the channel after hearing about the bear and cougar I had hoped he would offer one of the cabins but no such luck. Larry had a couple of beers and I chatted to him for a bit he liked my story so far and was interested in the trip. He took a few pictures of me in the kayak and promised to post them on the blog.

So I made off before it got too dark. There was a narrow channel I could take to get back to the inside passage route to Alaska, and it would save me some time and effort. After the bear and cougar stories and the worried look on the guys' faces, I was for the first time a bit scared about camping that night. I didn't find the place to camp but I did find a really wee island about 100 square meters so set up camp there.

Also a first: the mosquitos. They were everywhere, eating me alive. It must have been because I was a lot further inland that was the only difference from all my other campsites. It was getting dark quick and I had a monster of a day kayaking so it was a quick dinner, rice with chicken stock and cheese sauce, very simple meals to make but really quick and substantial. That night was dodgy. There was a seal that seemed to not like me being there on the island and kept splashing around. To an overactive mind it sounded like a bear jumping into the water to come and get me. I lay in the hammock very alert, listening for the imaginary bear to claw its way up the rocks. I was keen to get the hell away from that place. I had the serious heebie-jeebies.

I was up at first light, no breakfast, and away as quick as possible. The weather was damp and miserable, it was a tight channel and a feeling like I was being

watched never left me. It was strange how it all affects you, the bear and cougar stories and the sudden closed in feeling really unnerved me.
I had to stop for breakfast though and picked a spot at the end of the channel where it opened up into Fitzhugh Sound. I was still unnerved though and was looking over my shoulder every two minutes thinking a bear or cougar was trying to sneak up on me. The day was very cold and windy so the only way to keep warm was to keep
kayaking, no rest for the wicked.

Chapter Three
The Old Man and the Sea

I was hoping to see some Orcas, but so far nothing.
But nature did have a wee treat for me. There were
about 100 eagles lining the trees all within about 200
meters, I counted 16 in one tree. This was unreal. I
presumed eagles were solitary animals, apart from
ones with young. I believe they must have been
waiting for bait balls, where whales or gannets force
small fish into a tight ball in the water and feed on
them.

They were having no luck though and looked just
as miserable as I felt, poor things. I picked a wee
island again but this time I was in an open channel
and felt a lot better. But my defensive strategy, which
I had thought up the night before for waiting cougars
and bears hiding in the woods as I landed, was to
charge the forest line waving my paddle and shouting
as if I could see them. I felt this was a cunning plan
and would scare a horde of Klingons off. Although
anybody seeing this might think I was of my head but
that's the beauty of being in the middle of nowhere:
nobody to judge you on your seemingly crazy actions.
I got some fishing done but was having no luck
whatsoever. This was becoming a big problem. I was
constantly hungry. The oats were a lifesaver. I really
looked forward to them every morning, but I needed
meat. I dreamt of meat every night! Mmm cheese
burgers, sausages and juicy steaks.

The next day was miserable again but I felt I could make it to Namu, which I did, it was an old fish cannery. There was a dock with three boats moored up and old buildings all around. In its day, 2,000 people lived and worked here but now the forest had reclaimed 90% of it and the rest was falling down. There were two caretakers, Rene and Pete, who looked over it and were helpless to stop it as it fell to bits. I was allowed to set up camp in one of the hangers and I mingled with the boaters and fishermen who were passing through. It was an interesting place. I got to walk through and see all the old machinery and what was left of the shop. It was all closed down in the '90s and the forest and ocean were quickly taking it all back.

There was a big floating hut the caretakers had built for everyone to eat in, as all the boaters and staff would group together and have a big potluck for dinner. I got invited in and it was great. There was crab, salmon, chicken, shrimp, pasta all cooked to perfection. I kind of felt embarrassed as I didn't have anything to contribute to the potluck. My cooking at the best of times is only just bearable to me! But everybody was keen to hear about my trip and my quest for Alaska. There was a group of sailing friends who were on a similar journey to mine, but sailing. During my stay at Namu the weather was terrible and I was glad to

be somewhere out of the rain. It rained for a further two days, so I stayed. My time was spent quizzing the fishermen on how to catch salmon and what to use. I also studied their filleting technique. I told them how crap a fisherman I was who could only catch the odd rockfish. They told me the rockfish were real good eating and all I needed to do was jig for them. So I set about practicing off the dock and wow!! I caught 15 rockies in about an hour. All small ones but I could easy make a meal out of them if I had too.

The sport fishermen would be out all day trying to catch salmon and halibut, but were having no luck. They got mostly big rockfish, which they were happy with, apart from one of them who really wanted salmon. While I was practicing jigging off the dock I got a big one! As I was pulling it up there was a flash of silver, it was a salmon. I got real excited and was shouting for a net to land it.

Pulled it out and weighed it on the scales: seven and a half pounds. I was elated as now I had something to put into the potluck and the girls offered to cook it up for me too! There was a spring in my step! It was the first salmon caught off the dock that year and I had great delight telling the fishermen when they came back, and one spent his every spare minute fishing off the dock after that, but he had no luck. I got to watch the guys filleting the fish; it was interesting to watch. They could fillet the fish without gutting them. It was good I was learning to fish and how to fillet, I could not have landed in a better place in the rain. At night we would swap stories, the fishing buddies were from Bella Coola and the skipper of the boat used to be a tugboat driver. He told me about one time passing through Campbell River in a storm. He was pulling a barge full of digging equipment and there was a guy watching the load on the barge. The guy radioed him telling him to come back and rescue him as the barge was going down, he managed to get there just in time as the guy jumped to safety and they broke the lines as the barge went down swallowed up by the water. A few weeks later investigators sent some divers down to discover what happened. They discovered a log had been caught in a whirlpool and it rammed into the side of the barge ripping a hole in it.

Apparently fishing boats have disappeared in that area seemingly swallowed up and spat out further down the channel. I might have picked a different route if I had known all that!

Namu was an interesting place you met all kinds of people, everyone from a hermit who lived in the wilderness and came by to help out on the dock from time to time. I think he liked to talk to real people now and again. Right the way through the different classes of people up to the classy big expensive boats with owners who were loud and obnoxious, but everybody joined in with the potluck and enjoyed themselves.

There was a whale forming bait balls in the bay that evening and the eagles were feasting on them. So was every other animal able to swim or fly. It'squite a spectacular sight: you have a whale splashing around, sea gulls going nuts, diving loons, and eagles getting in on the feast.

The sun came out the next day so I took my chance and headed off. But I could have easily spent the rest of the summer in Namu. Pete was talking about building another float to give them more space and it would have been great to help with the project. But Alaska was still whispering in my ear "Danny, Danny come on!"

I said my goodbyes and set off for Bella Bella. Once I got out of the bay and into the main channel there were Humpback whales all over, but they were all far away. None came close. The views were amazing. I was blown away, big mountains that just seemed to just roll on back into the distance forever with little fluffy clouds above them and a calm blue ocean. The sheer scale and vastness of the area made it feel real special.

As I entered the next channel that would take me to Bella Bella I decided to try some fishing and camp up. This time I fished from the kayak, just jigging off the side and caught three flatfish ranging from two to three pounds. I chose to believe they were small halibut, but more than likely another type of flatfish. But there was no one around to argue with me so in my mind they were halibut. Caught a few rockfish and what appeared to be a Pollock. Luckily for them the halibut was enough for my dinner, and boy were they tasty!

It was a popular channel, there were a lot of boats and tugs pulling big barges full of steel containers going through the channel, but I slept well. I had gotten over my heebie-jeebies and was back to believing bears were just like people, most are good but there is the odd bad bugger, but if I was lucky I wouldn't meet him and cougars wouldn't attack a full grown man unless they were injured and desperate.

It was day 26 and I headed for Bella Bella.

Typical, as I was crossing the channel a tug and barge came around the corner and headed straight for me. I had to paddle like a maniac to get out the way. I was making my way around a corner when I saw movement on the beach. I steered the kayak in that direction and just floated in, it was a large black wolf. He was sniffing around a big rock and didn't notice me. As I got closed I noticed it wasn't a rock at all it was a dead Sea lion and he was having a nibble. Then he noticed me and trotted back a bit looking over his shoulder. As I got closer he pulled back into the tree line and turned to face me, watching me but obviously not wanting to pass up on such a big prize. He was nothing like wolfs you see on the TV. He was scruffy looking, long legs with a black back, and extremely intelligent looking watchful eyes. The closer I got the more he would back up into the woods but always looking at me with those hungry eyes. I considered setting up camp on a wee island opposite as I was sure the carcass would attract more wildlife, but I was hungry too and Bella Bella had a supermarket!

I left him to his feast as I planned to have my own very soon. Kayaking up the channel to Bella Bella there were two kayakers coming the other way but on the other side of the channel. I considered going across to tell them of the wolf but decided to let him gorge in peace.

Bella Bella was quite a big town and coming up talking to different people they all gave me different advice. Some said stay away from Bella Bella as it was a rough native town and I should go to Shearwater about 5km away, others told me not to go to Shearwater as it was an overpriced posh settlement. I just stopped at the first place I came to which happened to be Bella Bella. There were a lot of boats in the dock but I managed to find a spot to tie up on, got the basics at the supermarket, and treated myself to a pack of sausages and loaf of bread and some butter. I had done all my kayaking in a three-quarter length wet suit and this was what I walked around in. One guy asked me if it was laundry day; my reply was "it was laundry day a long long time ago."

Nearly four weeks and I had only managed to get two showers. I reasoned the rain kept me clean and anyway 99 per cent of the time there was nobody to smell me. I managed to hunt down a public phone and called up Lisa and Matt in Vancouver. People had been updating my blog and Larry had even sent in a few pictures, which was great.

I didn't look for anywhere to stay. I was much more happy being in the woods on my own now, might off been turning into a bit of a hermit myself. So I just packed the new supplies and headed off into the distance in my trusty kayak. There were lots of boats coming and going from Bella Bella and I wondered what it would be like growing up in such an isolated place.

It was a nice day again; I could get used to this. Seeing all the boats in the area, I felt sorry for the people on them. Yeah they get to see the beauty of the places but the feeling you get when you put some effort into getting to these places is immense; you get a great feeling of satisfaction and a lot more time to take it all in. It felt like these moments would always belong to me and I would forever be able to remember the contentment and satisfaction I was feeling.

I found a wee secluded beach for my lunch and couldn't wait to tuck into those sausages. Wow I don't think sausages have ever tasted so good, they were delicious smothered in butter and wrapped in the bread. Mmm sausage butties, you can't beat them! It was a treat and I deserved it.

I was enjoying the sun but the tide was coming in and I wanted to get further up the channel to cross it if I could. It would be my second big open crossing and I wanted to be at the narrowest point to do it as there was no protection from the full swell.

However the wind and tide had other plans, I had to battle up the coast hugging the shoreline. There was no way I was going to attempt the crossing so I found a sheltered bay. There were two sailboats in the bay, too, so I wasn't the only one hiding.

Didn't need to fish as I was fully supplied up, but the girls at Namu told me they go beachcombing a lot as you can find all sort of things. They had found a few glass balls the Japanese fishermen use to keep their nets up, so my beachcombing started, but with no immediate luck.

The next morning the weather was good again, so I made my way across the opening and up a wee narrow channel that opened up into a big basin. I had to weave my way through lots of small islands so it was back to keeping my eye out for tree climbing cougars.

Stopped for lunch on a real nice pebbly beach and enjoyed more sausage butties, the sun was hot and life was real good. Onward and upwards, I had a long day kayaking but the weather changed towards the end of the day. It was hard work finding a good campsite, so hard I had to settle for a bug-infested swamp. I had misplaced my bug spray so I was getting eaten alive again.

Next day was wet, foggy and cold I made my way up to Jackson Narrows as coming through there would bring me out right in front of the crossing for a town called Klemtu. Jackson Narrows is a provincial park and very nice and fast flowing, but I was shocked to see two big noisy fish farms in it. I did not understand just how the government allows fish farms next to such beautiful places; I suppose it's just a dot on a map to them. I stopped for lunch at a wee beach and for the first time saw four dead starfish. I don't know if the fish farm is

responsible; all I know is I had not seen dead starfish on any other beach I had been on. As I was crossing over the channel to Klemtu a seaplane buzzed right over the top of me, did a big turn, and up Jacksons Narrows to land. Glad he saw me, I thought he was going to land right on top of me!

I just stopped off in Klemtu to fill up with some water as I hadn't passed any good streams in the past couple of days. But I was very tempted to go into the supermarket for more sausages! However, I resisted temptation and continued on with my journey. Further up on my right there were around five bright red and white buildings that appeared to be a lighthouse and maybe a coastguard station. It made a nice change as all else I could see was the ocean and about 20 feet up the shoreline before the fog obliterated everything else.

The kayaking was easy though and I made good distance. There was nothing to see or do so I had an early night with the thoughts of getting to Butedale the next day. Butedale was on my map and I figured it was another town like Klemtu. How wrong I was.

Pulling on the cold wet wetsuit in the morning was the worst thing about mornings and I would always leave it to the end just before I jumped into the kayak. I was off really early that morning; in the water by 6

am. The weather was still miserable and I had to stick close to the shoreline just to see it. The weather quickly deteriorated and it started hammering down with rain, and the wind was turning the waves into whitecaps. It was not pleasant to be out in this weather. By 11 o'clock I needed to find a camp but there was no place to take shelter. I was in a rocky corridor with sheer cliffs on each side. There were places I could get to but the wind and waves made it too difficult to stop and unload safely. One o'clock and I was still looking but by now my hands were freezing and I couldn't touch my thumb and pinkie together. This was a bad sign and if I didn't find shelter soon I might not be able to sort my camp out and cook food. So I picked a place where the waves where not too bad. I had to drag the kayak up steep rocks fully loaded. I quickly set up my tarp and hammock, boiled some water for a hot chocolate, stripped off, and jumped into my
sleeping bag in the hammock. A fire would have been nice but all the wood was soaked and it takes a lot of effort to find the dry stuff and keep it dry, so the plan was to sit it out and warm myself up.
It never stopped raining all day and night. The mountains were alive with waterfalls. There must have been 12 cascading down the mountain opposite me. I was a relieved man the next morning. It was calm and clear.
Butedale was not far away either. Only about 30 minutes kayak and I found a great campsite just 10 more minutes up the channel. Bloody typical! Looks like my luck had finally said "you're on your own son." Made it to Butedale and there was a big wide thundering waterfall right beside it. The

place looked a real wreck. It was another old Cannery and it was in a lot worse state than Namu. It didn't look too safe but there was a sign saying homemade ice cream, and I figured I needed to get some local info on what lay ahead, so decided to stop off. There was an old dude staying there called Lou. He was looking after the place by himself. He offered to let me stay in the houses further up, but I think he was going to charge me so I said I would just put my hammock up. He was living in the big building that had not fallen down yet. Lou had an artistic streak and spent his time burning pictures onto wood with a soldering iron. Eccentric would be the best word to describe Lou. Obviously very hardy to be living out here, but funny how he wouldn't shut up. Suppose he didn't get many visitors, although he said he had a guy stay with him most of the time but he was away shopping and he wished he wasn't going to come back! There was electricity but there didn't seem to be a generator. When I asked him about it, he was dead keen to show me. When the factory had been up and running there was a big water turbine supplying all the electricity. But only the water wheel worked now. He had set up a truck alternator to it and a converter that supplied all his needs; but the water used to be directed into the wheel via a big wooden pipe that was now broken and spouting water everywhere. So he had built wooden channels to catch all the water and direct it to the wheel. It was a big maze of fast moving water tracks and dams. I loved it! It reminded me of playing on the beach as a boy and directing small streams through the sand. I used to spend ages building sand dams. He must have

spent ages constructing it and maintaining it all, and he leapt
about from bank to bank like a mountain goat, in spite of the fast moving water. I sat listening to his stories. He told me about a 22-year-old woman who rowed to Alaska in 1937, I was not the only crazy person to do a journey like this, it seemed there were crazier!

I quizzed him about any hot springs in the area as I felt could do with a good soak. There were two, I had just passed one but it was hard to find; then there was a more popular one a bit further up. He recommended the ones I had just passed and gave me directions to it but I didn't trust him. The reason I didn't quite trust him was he claimed to never have heard of Scotland and made me show him on a map and explain that it was north of England. I believe he was trying to play the hermit totally separate from the real world, but I could see in his eyes he was full of shit. The hot springs further up seemed like a safe bet, Bishop Bay. He was also telling me about a spirit bear that visited the beach now and again but I took this with a pinch of salt until he showed me a home movie of it on the beach! After that I could hardly stop my eyes scanning the beach all the time.

That night I was glad I had camped outside near the ocean, not only because the cabin he offered was a mouse infested damp hole, but there was a Humpback whale and calf across the channel and late evening the mother was singing. The sound was amplified with the high mountains on either side. It sounded so good with very deep long notes. Before this I thought you could only pick up whales singing through underwater microphones, what a very pleasant surprise.

Next morning I packed up early as the night before Lou had offered to make me breakfast before I headed off: sausage meat and fried potato. But when I saw him it became quite clear there would be no breakfast as he was totally avoiding the subject and just wanted to haver (talk nonsense). I think I had got all his good stories out and was left with the crap. So I decided I was better off on my way and stop for Breakfast further up as all my stuff was packed. He said I could make it to the hot springs the same day as it was only 20 miles away. Coming out of Butedale I decided to cross over to the north side of the channel, as I would need to for the springs. I was trolling a fishing lure out the back of the kayak, this time using a heavier lure like the guys at Namu suggested. I had the rod wedged down the back of my life vest and the line started going out but I thought it was just another bit of seaweed since I was getting very good at catching the stuff. Until the salmon leapt from the water! I got very excited and reeled it in. It was my first fish from trolling and I switched the camera on to record it so people would believe me. I let it play about until I had my net out and everything set up. When I first attempted to get it in the net, it took off and I thought I had lost it. It was two seconds of disbelief but no it was still on and I managed to net it the second time.

I was delighted with the catch it provided a bit of excitement from the usual hum drum of paddling all day. I was advised in the fishing shop in Vancouver to store the fish in a bag and drag it in the water behind the kayak but I found this a bad idea as it caused a lot of drag, so in the kayak it went.

It was dull but not rainy and I made my way to Bishop Bay hot springs very happy. Lou said the springs can get busy and as it was Friday I thought there was a good chance it would be but I was hoping to have them all to myself. As I paddled up the channel I could see boats coming the other way and it looked like they were all heading to the same place. I was willing them to be going somewhere else, as I was looking forward to relaxing and eating my prize fish in peace and quiet and then going for a nice soak in the springs. The last thing I wanted was a big group of teenyboppers partying and making a ruckus. Anyway I saw three boats speed in, heading for the springs and I followed them in. I was very nervous for some reason and a big group of people seemed like my worst nightmare, I think I really was turning into some kind of anti-social hermit.

There was a small dock with two boats tied up to it and another sailboat tied up to a buoy. I got talking to some people on the dock who said there were some campsites a couple of hundred meters down. There was decking built for tents to camp on and I easily hung up my hammock over the deck. It didn't take me long to unpack and get my swim shorts on and head for the springs. Luckily there was a wee pool to wash yourself in before you jumped into the main spring, as I needed a good scrub!

After the springs, I cooked up the salmon. I wrapped it in tinfoil and grilled it on a fire while I made the rice and mixed up my favourite sauce. I was stuffed; it didn't stop me from going for a second dip in the hot springs though. It was pure luxury to be soaking in the hot water after all the bad miserable weather.

I met a family on a boat tied to the dock, the Barrett family on the Wild Fire boat. They were on a fishing trip and used the springs as their base. They were a good bunch of people and it was good swapping stories, me with my kayak trip and their adventures on the boat. They did tell me that they wouldn't attempt the crossing into Alaska in their boat, never mind a kayak! My anti-social fears were unfounded I got chatting to everybody.

I decided to take the next day off and do some fishing and soaking, didn't have much luck fishing but loads of soaking! When the Wild Fire came back in Marla invited me to dinner. She had burgers and after our conversations the night before she knew they were a favourite of mine. I have what most people consider very strange eating habits. I do not eat most cooked vegetables, I actually hate them and find them disgusting. Raw is fine but as soon as their cooked, yuck! However, I love meat: sausages, burgers, steak and it was all I craved. So much so that I used to doze off in the hammock daydreaming about a bear attacking me
so I would have to kill it and it would be a shame to waste all that meat so I would have to strip it and eat it.

When I was bored of the kayaking I would ponder ways of preserving as much meat as
possible. Food filled most of my waking day and my dreams! I knew I was eating enough food as I was always eating but I was also burning lots of calories.

It was great mingling with all the people passing

through the springs, everybody said it was the worst summer in years and the old timers at Namu said it was the worst they had seen in 50 years of living on the coast, so much rain. I had made good time getting here though and it was apparently because of the bad weather, a north wind brings clear skies but then I would be fighting the wind all the time, whereas the south wind brings clouds and rain, so apparently I can't have it all ways on this trip. Quizzed the locals from Kitimat on cabins I could use as all my kit was wet or damp, drying them on the fire was no use as the air was so damp. They said if I continued around the Island there was one not too far away with a stove so I decided on that. But I had to have a quick dip in the morning before I left as who knows when I might get another chance to relax in a hot springs. As I made my way out the bay the boats passed me off on their next trip and more importantly said they would update my blog for me.

Not far around the corner and I spied the cabin in the woods. It had a nice gravel beach plus it was raining again so I stopped off. Cabins are simple out here just a hut with some bunk beds and a stove (all you really need). It was an old rusty stove but once she got going, let out a tremendous heat and my clothes were dry in no time. I got some fishing done off the rocks but didn't catch a thing, so just made some pasta for dinner.

After dinner I had a cast out onto the gravelly beach just for something to do and ended up catching three 2-3 pound fish. Ate most of them and made up the rest with rice for my lunch the next day. As I was updating my video diary, I caught some movement

out the corner of my eye. It was a mink making its way across the
beach. He stopped off and was sniffing about where I gutted the fish, but there was none left for him. I stayed as still as I could and he ran straight to me and by my feet. As I turned to keep the camera on him he noticed me and made a sharp turn to the woods, jumped on top of a log and stared at me. So I gave him a wave and he bounced off.

Set off the next morning in fair weather but as I got up around the corner of the Island the weather changed, and the wind got up. I had to battle to get anywhere as again there was no place to camp. Eventually found somewhere not too bad but it was raining heavy now, so I spent the rest of the day in the hammock. I didn't have any books with me. The only one I brought was on edible plants and it had got wet so I left it in a hut for someone else to dry out and read.

Most of the time I just daydreamed, I think I solved all the world's problems five times over but forgot to write them down!

Next day was no better but I did make it across a big channel before the weather got too bad.

Another salmon caught while trolling, but this time it was big, around 15 pounds, and too big for the net I had. So I struggled with it and tried to see if I could grab its tail but it was way too slimy. I knew sticking my fingers through its gills would work but the hook was in its jaw and I didn't want to risk impaling my finger. So I let it swim about till I landed the kayak. Once on shore it was easy to land, and he was going to keep me stocked in salmon for a few days.

Camp that night was very windy and wet but there was plenty of good firewood about. I cooked all the fish, which took a while; cooked it in four sections it was so big. I ate about a quarter of it and stored the rest. A storm came in and lasted all the next day so I stayed where I was and solved more of the world's problems.

There was a river near my camp and I was concerned bears might be about but I did have a good look around and there didn't seem to be any sign, which I found strange. Plenty of eagles just up the river looking for salmon but I didn't see any salmon in the river.

All my kit was soaked again so it was pointless stopping in the last hut. This was not what I was expecting on the trip. Yeah, I knew it would be hard and I looked forward to the challenge. This however was not hard, you just had to tolerate it, which I could do but boy was it boring.

The wind had died down but it was still raining the next day so I headed off, made some good distance but it was not enjoyable. By now I just wanted to get to Alaska as fast as possible. If the weather was going to be like this I was best getting it over and done with. For all that I was seeing I would be as well sitting on a rower facing a blank wall all day.

Weather got bad again so I found a camp and hid again. I was eating a lot of salmon as my rice was running low. This is not a good idea as salmon is quite high in protein and gave me the runs; lots of crapping in the woods!

The rain was real bad and it lasted all night, the wind had loosened my tarp and the water collected in it till it was too heavy and collapsed, soaking all my equipment. I was safe in my hammock but there was nothing I could do. If I got out I would get soaked in the middle of

the night so I just waited to investigate in the morning. At first light it was a wet soggy mess and still raining. I just thought that's it, I quit. This is bollocks.

There was no point. There is just so much camping in the rain a man can take. No wonder I had seen very little wildlife; even the Orcas were hiding from the rain. Now I thought how do I quit? Turning back would mean a week's kayak to Kitimat, forward would mean two days to

Prince Rupert. So quitting meant carrying on, if I made it to PR then I would be in the home straight for Alaska! All right, I would keep going but if it got worse, all bets were off.

As I made my way up, some yachts were coming the other way and appeared to move to intercept me. It was some of the people I met at Namu. Four yachts, and as each one passed they shouted encouragement to me, and the last one slowed down enough to throw me a beer! This random meeting perked me right up; I was instantly 100 times more determined to make it to Alaska. I celebrated with salmon curry and beer. Ah, life was good!

Chapter Four
Insomnia

I was headed for Porcher Island at the end of the Grenville Channel to a wee town called Oona River.

As I crossed the open water I caught another salmon but this one was different it was a pink salmon about five pounds and I got him into the net fine and clobbered him well, and as I was putting him into my bag to store him, I had to grab my rod as I thought it was going to fall off the kayak. When I went to put the fish bag away it was empty! The fish had slipped out. I was gutted. Oh well, easy come easy go, but I didn't have a lot of grub left and was counting my lucky stars when I landed it.

I made it to Oona River and optimistically asked the people on the dock if there was a shop. They laughed and said the nearest was Prince Rupert. I told them the story of losing my supper on the way in and Mike asked if I was Scottish and then he and his wife invited me to dinner, as they had been fishing and had plenty.

They also invited me to stay on the boat for the night too, which made life a lot easier as I would have needed to camp in the woods across the water. They also had a friend and daughter who were passing through for dinner. The food was great! Loved the way they cooked the salmon, just cut it into steaks and slapped it onto the barbecue. Mike is an ocean biologist and his friend was a creek walker. He would walk up remote creeks counting salmon every year. It was great quizzing him on bears as he must have come across quite a few. He did always take a shotgun with him but had only ever fired one warning shot. For a man to walk in the territory of feeding bears and only ever fire one warning shot to scare off a bear who seemed to be stalking him, I thought this backed up my belief that most bears were good and not going to bother me. Both guys had grown up in the fishing community and had been fishermen most of their lives. So the discussions about how to conserve and sustainably harvest fish stocks were great. I was learning all about the fishing industry on the BC coast and now had a better reason to dislike the fish farms I had seen on the way up, which had rudely disturbed my peace and tranquillity with their noisy generators.

Apparently they're all Atlantic salmon fish, a foreign species to the Pacific coast, and escaped fish bring a disease to the local Pacific salmon and many believe it's decimating the native species. The local fishermen are restricted on where and when they can fish to conserve fish stocks, but the area is on the border with Alaska and the US fishermen have no restrictions. So the Americans sit just outside the Skeena River outlet where all the salmon have to pass through taking as much as they want when the Canadians have their hands tied. Wow, I was discovering there was a bit of animosity towards the fisherman from each country, but not only that – America and Canada are still arguing over the exact border between the two. This surprised me, as you would think they'd have it all sorted out by now. We spent the night debating the ins and outs over alcohol-laced coffee. I had forgotten how much I loved a good debate and how much I loved learning about things you just wouldn't hear about if you were a sightseeing tourist on a cruise ship.

Anyway it was getting late and time to head to bed. John was leaving early the next morning and he threw me a couple of sides of smoked salmon for my trip, which was greatly appreciated. That night I could not sleep and was baffled about it until I remembered I had not drunk tea or coffee in six weeks and the coffee had hit me harder than the alcohol!

The local community was having a bakery sale the next day so I decided to hang around as I had developed a sweet tooth on this trip. After a pleasant night on the Oona Maid I met a guy on the dock named Lutz who had lots of kayaks and the one he had on the dock had a Scottish flag on it and he explained there was a Scottish couple passing through some years ago on the same trip as me who he bought the kayak from after their journey. He invited me to the community coffee and cake at 10, and showed me where the community centre was where I could use the computer.

It was day 40 and the first time I had used a computer but it was dial up and extremely slow. But I did get to update my spotthescot blog for everyone.

I ended up at the coffee and cake community meet up which was great I got to meet the locals, seasonal residents and all year ones, but the community spirit was great. Everybody seemed very excited about the kids doing the bakery sale later at 12, and so was I.

Bumped into Mike and got invited up for a lunchtime sandwich. Wow, these guys sure know how to look after strangers! We headed down to the bakery sale and as we got there seven minutes late there were loads of people coming out with mountains of cakes piled on their plates and there were only a few bits and bobs left over. Wow, it must have been a feeding frenzy!

I got invited to come and check out the fish hatchery up the road. They were building a new cabin with some help from some uni students, and there was a beach bonfire and potluck later.

Lutz offered to let me use his bicycle, but warned me the gears were a bit wonky, to go and visit the hatchery which I did but found no one there so just toured around a bit. It was a nice day for cycle but the wind always seemed to be threatening to blow some rain clouds over. Oona River is gorgeous and the people are great. I felt a bit guilty as I didn't really have anything to trade for this great hospitality.

The food at the potluck was amazing; there was Sockeye salmon, crab, shrimp and chicken. Mmm, I was getting treated! After at the bonfire there were some fireworks for the kids. I dug out my fire poi balls, which were soaking from sitting at the bottom of my kayak for a few weeks, but I got them dried out and gave the kids a wee fire spinning show. It felt good to feel like I was giving something back even if it was just

a wee bit of entertainment.

I spent another night on the Oona Maid but the next day it was time to get going. Would have loved to stay and help out on the cabin at the hatchery but Alaska was still calling and now it was real loud! In the morning the tide was out and the dock at Oona almost completely dries up so I decided to wait and have one last go on the community computer, but wow was it slow!

Soon I was on my way though, my goal was to make it to Prince Rupert and stock up on food before my final push for Alaska.

As I made my way through the islands to the east of Porcher Island I decided to do some trolling and as I was paddling along I noticed a dolphin just on my left so I slowed down to watch him. It looked like he was hunting, so I thought I better pull in my lure as I didn't want to catch a fish then have him bite into it! But disaster as I stopped, my lure sank to the bottom and got stuck; it was my most successful one too. It was just a heavy yellow weight that didn't look anything like a fish, but it was good, I lost it and the dolphin disappeared, probably laughing at me.

Because I didn't leave Oona River till 10:30 the wind was starting to pick up just as I needed to make a big crossing. The direct route was around the front of Smith Island but it was too windy, so I needed to take the back route which would take me up a fast moving channel if I timed it right the tide would be going in the same direction and I would make good time.

As I was crossing it was funny to witness firsthand what the fishermen were on about the night before. The Canadian fishing authority opens up fishing in sectors for a limited time and each boat has to obey certain rules, only use one size of net and it's only allowed in the water for 30 minutes at a time. So you get about 10 boats all darting about with one fisheries boat timing them. It was an interesting scenario. I decided to hide my rod as I had not bothered to get a fishing licence as it would have cost me over 100 bucks, and I was just fishing for food. I would like to have seen them try to board me and search my vessel, but decided not to tempt them!

It seemed to take forever to get across in the wind but I got across to Smith Island in the end and started to make my way around the back. The wind seemed to be coming around the back of the Island, too, which was disheartening, but the tide was changing soon so I carried on hoping it would cancel out the wind. I started passing old houses and cabins on the Island. I was tempted to give up the kayaking and see if I could find a cosy place for the night until I started hearing gun shots coming from up ahead. It turned out to be a father and son doing a bit of target practice. I said hi as I passed and they asked where I was going and suggested I stop off at a well-known camping area on an Island up ahead.

Further up I came across another family just docking who were going to be staying on their holiday home for the week and quizzed me a bit. I got the feeling they wouldn't mind quizzing me some more but I was shy and felt keen to be on my way, and maybe even back into the wilderness?

There seemed to be people everywhere. I had talked to more people in the last two days than I had the whole trip.

As I continued around the Island it became apparent that the wind was too strong for the tide and I had to stick close into the Island to keep out of the worst of it. But there was nowhere to stop and on the other side there was another old cannery, but a well preserved one with houses and a road. I decided to get over there and find a camp spot and see if I could hitchhike into town. I battled across the channel and set up camp and headed for the road. I passed a sign saying private land of Inverness Properties No Trespassing!

But as I was Scottish and spent some of my youth living in the City of Inverness, decided I was exempt, or well, I could talk my way out of it anyway.

There were not a lot of cars on the road but a woman in a camper had told me there was a shop in a town called Port Edward 5km up the road so I just hiked along the road. It was a small shop but not too expensive. I was very weary of running out of money so spent a long time trying to figure out what was the best value. Ended up with a big bag of rice and one of oats, a bag of bacon bits which was full of fat but I thought this would be good energy, plus I could use the fat to fry the fish in. I needed drinking chocolate as well and there were two tubs to choose from. Of course I chose the cheapest one. There was no luck hitching back and it was a long walk hungry and tired after a long day kayaking but I didn't have much choice. I was soon to discover my camping spot was the worse yet. There was a train track about 20 meters back from me. I hoped it was a rarely used one. But I do know bears like railway tracks in Canada for the grain that sometimes falls out of the containers. No problem with bears that night but I did get a visit of two very scrawny looking wolves. But when they saw me they took off in that funny way wolves trot, and at around two in the morning a freight train went past; it scared the utter crap out of me. I woke up totally disorientated wondering what the hell was going on.

Eventually it went past and I got back to sleep hoping there would not be another one!

Next day I set off and decided to give Prince Rupert a miss as I had my supplies. As I made my way to go around Digby Island the tide was out and there was only around eight inches of water. Instead of waiting for the tide to come in I paddled around looking for deeper channels, which I did end up finding. It was a nice day and it was a joy to paddle. As I came around the west side of Digby Island I came across a nice sandy beach so decided to stop for lunch, which was bacon sandwiches. Mmm Heaven. The whole area seemed to be very shallow water and I was having no luck fishing and in danger of losing all my lures.

I had a good day though and the weather was fantastic so I stopped off on a wee long Island, Got all my kit out to dry off and set up my camp

shower. It was a black plastic bag you fill with water and let the sun heat it. I had carried it from Vancouver for the last six weeks and this was the first time it was hot enough to use it. Once the water was warmish I hung it up on a tree and showered. This was how I envisioned the whole trip and was amazed that the further north I got the warmer it was getting! I could see the mountains of Alaska in the distance; I judged I could make it in a day or two. It was great to see Alaska and be so close to my goal, I had decided getting to Alaska would be mission accomplished and whatever happened after didn't matter as I would have done what I set out to do.

It seemed that a lot of my plans in life had failed; I had left school at 15 to get ready to join the army, which I had already signed up for. Teachers advised me to do my exams but I was going to be in the army for the rest of my life and didn't need silly exams. But I only spent a year in training before getting kicked out, due to my shoulder dislocating a couple of times. At the age of 23 I discovered boxing, which became my passion and I was determined to be the best. Disaster struck again when in the East District Championship I dislocated my shoulder in the ring twice. First time it popped out I managed to pull it back into place and a worried looking referee let me continue. But when it popped out again I tried to hide it from the ref but the audience's screams alerted him and it

was game over.

I knew completing this journey would be a massive physiological step forward for me, and once I could see the goal there was no stopping me. The wee island I was on made contact with the mainland at low tide and a massive sand/mud area opened up so I spent an hour searching for crabs. I was told they hid under the sand and you could dig them up but I had no luck.

I left in the morning at high tide and it was another gorgeous day. I hoped to get to Hecate Strait and camp there before tackling the big crossing into Alaska the next morning. I stopped off for lunch which was more bacon sandwiches and two kayakers appeared coming the other way. A man and woman who had kayaked down from Glacier Bay and were headed to the gulf Islands south of Vancouver Island. They quizzed me on camping sites and maps and as you might already guess I wasn't the best guy to ask! They said they had enjoyed some good weather so far which seemed the exact opposite from me. They were well equipped and seemed like a very nice couple and I don't want to know what they thought of my set up. There was no way I was pulling out my maps! There were a lot of sport fishermen in the area and one bunch of guys threw me a beer. I stashed it away to keep for my celebration drink when I hit Alaskan soil. I stopped and did some fishing; just a little jigging and caught two good sized flatfish; just enough for dinner.

I made camp with Alaska firmly in sight knowing that the next day I would be there!

I was excited the next morning but it was really foggy, Packed up and hung around until I could see the other side and then headed off. It was a big crossing but there was no wind, which was good, and as I got to the other side the sport fishermen were back at it so I decided to do a little fishing of my own and within about five minutes I had one, but this time it was a steelhead which is really from the trout family, he was only about five pounds so I kept on fishing and got another steely straight away. That was it; put the rod away for the day and I continued along. There was one more crossing before Alaska, but not as big. I crossed it and weaved my way through some islands to find a

floating camp for fishing boats with a massive star spangled banner flying, I had made it!!!

I spoke to the guys on the float and they directed me to a sandy beach I could camp at. They also offered me two sides of smoked steelhead but I said it was okay I had just caught two! As soon as I paddled away I was kicking myself for not accepting the fish.

A few weeks ago I had told myself to always accept food as you never know, but I am the worst ever at accepting charity. The fog had never really lifted and it started raining so
I called it a day and found the camp. Set up under a big tree and cooked the fish and drank the beer! I was a very happy man.
I had done it; made it to Alaska under my own power in a kayak. There was a great feeling of accomplishment and of astonishment. It was hard for me to believe I had done it. I was so used to getting nearly there and never fully achieving my goals in life. Getting here changed that.
Ketchikan was next, however I didn't know how it was going to play out, as I was very low on money and it would soon disappear in a town.
The next day was going to be a potential tough one as it was again exposed to the full swell of the ocean at Dixon Entrance and up Revillagigedo Channel but it turned out to be a really nice day. I made great time and distance. A Humpback whale got quite close too, and caught some good sized rock cod. It had been a long day and I had travelled about 25 miles (40k) found a poor campsite but I was too tired to go on so made it do.
I hoped to find a stream for water but there was none. I did find lots of bear poop though, some fresh! I also done some beach combing as there was a old fishing boat wreck smashed all over the beach and found a whole glass ball the Japanese/Chinese use to keep their fishing nets afloat.
I had bought some waffle mix which I planned to make waffles with but ended up just adding it to

my bread/bannock mix and decided to use it as a batter for the fish and fry the Rock cod in the bacon fat. I was amazed how good it tasted, battered fish that tasted like bacon. Mmm, I was a genius. Move over Gordon Ramsay there's a new guy in town!

But I discovered that the tub of cheap hot chocolate was not hot chocolate, it was chocolate icing. But I decided to try it as hot chocolate and it turned out tasting better than the real stuff!

I was dead tired and set up a big fire to keep any bears away; if any did come by I slept right through it as I fell asleep at 8pm and did not stir till 6am, which was highly unusual for me.

It was a good night's sleep and I set off early the next morning, I needed to stop at the first stream for water and it was not far and a real nice beach. If I had just continued the day before by 30 minutes! I was tempted to set camp as it was such a nice day. There were blue skies with just little fluffy clouds above the mountains but something told me there would be a better beach further up and I wanted to do some fishing.

I got a nice Coho salmon and a nice Greenling cod then came across a beautiful white sandy beach. It was perfect!

It was only 11 o'clock and I set up camp. There was a tree that had fallen down onto the beach but was suspended about six feet above the sand and I decided to hang my hammock on it

as it was quite stable. It was by far the best placement of my hammock the whole trip. After my camp was sorted I stripped off and had a nap on the beach, life is good. I was very relaxed. Without the need to get anywhere there was a good feeling in me where there was nowhere for me to be and I could just enjoy the time alone in this wonderful place. When you have been on your own for a long time life seems so simple and stress free and I was enjoying it! I suppose being a daydreamer it makes it easy as I was never lonely.

A ferry/cruise ship went passed off in the distance and I imagine everyone looking out at my beach and wishing they could walk along the white sand paradise. I felt like I was now the luckiest man on the planet.

I was well rested and it was funny how I was looking forward to finding a great place to camp up for a few days and just relax, but when I found it all I wanted to do was see what's around the next corner! So off I went the next day. Again I caught a nice cod and after crossing a big channel against the wind I found a sheltered bay. I saw a kid fishing of the bank so had a cast and hooked a big Coho salmon. I had to go onshore to land it.

The kid was there with his father on a camping trip, they told me it was called Coho Cove. They were just waiting for a boat to come and pick them up and offered me the last of their supplies which was a few chocolate bars, two eggs, some buns and a tin of Spam, and a pint of milk, I offered them the salmon as it was a bit big for me but they wouldn't take it. When they got picked up the guy picking them up (Chuck) offered to let me park up my kayak on his dock in Ketchikan and if I needed I could sleep in one of his sheds. He might be able to help me find some casual work if I wanted it. As I was running out of money this was like a dream come true. So far everybody I met in Alaska had offered me food and

help. They left me to camp and I had a feast! There
was no saving anything. I gobbled everything up.
I looked forward to getting to Ketchikan now and
set off early the next morning. Paddling into the
town was an experience. The place was a lot
bigger than I had imagined and the fancy boats
were astonishing. Boats with helicopters and
speed boats on the back, and then the humongous
cruise ships. I found Chuck's dock and tied up but he
was not around and the girl in charge knew nothing
about me coming and looked at me as if I was a total
weirdo. I asked if there was somewhere I could get
changed and freshen up and she directed me to a
bathroom. When I looked in the mirror I understood
the look in her face. I looked like a salty sea dog. Hair
was everywhere along with the beard, and my hair
was three colours: ginger, grey, and bleached blond
on top. The girl ended up being super nice and
showed me around Ketchikan and when I discovered
that you could not exchange Canadian money to US
dollars anywhere in the town unless you had an
account
with the local bank, she managed to change it for me.
However the offer to stay in the shed was a no go as it
was tiny and in high use. So Chuck directed me to his
friend who had a hostel.
Eagle View Hostel was run and owned by a
pretend-grumpy old man. Dale was a bit of a
character. He worked all day taking out tourists in
small boats, fishing for halibut and rockfish. I
believe it was a strain on him being ultra-nice to
the paying customers all day so he tried to take it
out on everyone else. Once you saw through this it
was funny and he was a real good guy. He had

lived in Ketchikan all his life and was full of knowledge of the surrounding area. There was another kayaker staying there, too, and he told me about the Misty Fjords, an area not far from Ketchikan and I must have gone past the entrance on my way there. I told the kayaker about my trip and my kayaking experience before setting out and he thought I was mad and crazy but couldn't deny the fact that I had done it.

He was considering heading into the Misty Fjords but thought the 57 miles (90k) was too long and it scared him a bit. I tried to convince him it would be okay but he was having none of it. I think he did actually think I was off my head.

The next day I went looking for US Customs to declare myself. I went to the wrong federal building and they directed me to the right one with a quick phone call to say I was on my way. I expected to walk in and them ask me a few questions and pat me on the back when I explained that I had kayaked from Vancouver.

I spent the next five hours being grilled, fingerprinted, and criminal checked. At one point they said what I had done was no better than a Mexican running across the border (after, I thought I would have to be a pretty dumb Mexican to run across the border and head straight to US Customs!) However there were several problems. First up was a $5,000 fine for not declaring myself as soon as I docked in Ketchikan. It took me three days to get to Ketchikan once I had crossed the border; I failed to see the urgency. Apparently there were signs at every public dock to indicate this but I had come in on a private dock so didn't see one. I also needed a

pleasure craft visa for entering Alaskan water, $600, which of course I didn't have, and was shocked that my kayak is
classed the same as the big yachts and boats with helicopters on the back that I had seen on the way in. On top of all this there was no Canadian stamp on my passport. When I crossed over into Canada from America at Buffalo I was wearing my Scotland rugby top and the Canadian Customs guy ended up chatting to me about the highland games and how Nova Scotia had the biggest ones outside of Scotland, so he forgot to stamp my passport. So to the US Customs it looked like I had never left the US, so I had to go over my story again and again. They took me away and used every machine they could think off to fingerprint me, picture me, and criminal check me. They wanted physical proof that I had crossed into Canada at Buffalo, and hotel receipts in Canada, and I tried to explain they were not on my item list for my kayak journey.
I could not prove I had been in Canada until they asked to see my phone to check numbers and when I pulled it out, luckily it was a Rodgers phone that the US does not have. So that hurdle was crossed.
As for the $5,000 fine, they decided to let me off with it, as there was no sign at the dock I tied up to. The visa however was mandatory and I should have had it before coming and without it I would never be allowed back into the US. So they offered to give me it if I paid up. As you probably have already guessed I did not have the money for it. They did not know what to do with me, the customs guy dealing with me was trying his hardest to work around the rules to solve my problems but he had a job to do and

I got the feeling if he didn't do it right he would be patrolling the northernmost Artic border on foot. We came to a compromise: I would kayak back to Canada and he would give me the visa. He gave me three weeks to get out and report to Canadian Customs, just enough time to check out the Misty Fjords on my way out!

The nightmare was over and now my path was set, get back into the kayak and get paddling. It was a bit of a relief actually because Ketchikan was a tourist town that existed to entertain the cruise ships when they came in. It was pandemonium when one came in. There were ticket touts all over the place trying to get the tourists to go on their wild Alaskan day trips. Plus my money was low; my big brother Malky saved the day by sending 200 bucks, which helped a lot. So I stocked up and prepared to head off the next morning, I went to clean out my kayak. It had been sitting in the sun with the cover over it and when I pulled it off there was a pungent smell of fish. If bears have such a high sense of smell I should not be alive! I had forgotten to wash out my fish bag from the last time and it was inside the kayak.

That night I sat talking to Dale about my return trip and he suggested a few things and really thought instead of going to Prince Rupert I should head up Portland channel to Stewart/Hyder. I wasn't sure as I wanted (well, needed) to sell the kayak to get some money to return to Vancouver, and it would be easier to sell in the bigger town of PR, but I promised to give it more thought on my way out.

But it was time to go. The people I had met in

Ketchikan were good to me but I was glad to be on my way. I had visions of Navy Seals dropping out the sky to escort me out if I didn't get a move on.

It took me most of the morning to get my stuff sorted so I only made it to a camp a few miles out of Ketchikan. It was Chuck's camp, set up for his customers off the cruise ships. He had a company taking them out on fishing trips and after he would bring them to have their fish cooked for them in the camp.

In the morning the cook arrived to set up for the first batch of tourists. I had a good chat with her and a coffee but didn't want to hang around when the guests came although I'm sure they would have loved to grill me on the trip. But I wasn't in the mood to entertain. There were parts of the five hour interrogation I spent in customs that were very hard for me. I didn't like getting treated like a criminal and for the first two hours they kept an armed guard around until they decided I wasn't a threat. There were also some personal questions that really touched a nerve with me. Although they had done a lot for me in the end I wondered why the world had to be like this. Yes, you need rules, but surely common sense should be able to override some rules. I was never a threat and do not think I was the start of a massive influx of immigrants kayaking over the border from Canada to the American dream in Alaska.

As I made my way southward, Dale was coming back in with some clients and stopped off to wish me luck and quiz me if I was going up Portland Channel.

After he went passed the weather started to get worse with the wind picking up. Dale had told me about a

cabin on my way at Alva point at the entrance to the Misty Fjords and I really wanted to get to it, as the weather was bad. It was the worst weather and conditions I had been in the
whole trip. I went from paddling into big waves to trying to go along them but having to zigzag so I wasn't fully side-on to the big waves. I kept telling myself that it was crazy to be out in this weather but I was in a mood to push myself and the lure of the cabin was too great. It took a long time battling the wind and waves but I made it. The cabin was a cracker, too. There was a great oil stove in it that really heated the place up.

That evening I reflected on my day and quickly decided it was pure madness to be out in that water. I had told myself from the beginning that the trip was doable and easy so long as I didn't push it and paddle in stormy weather. On the plus side, the kayak rode the waves real good and it was a bit of a thrill bouncing up and down on them.

However it was extremely stupid and I would not be doing it again; if it got that bad I would not waste time in landing and setting camp.

Headed off the next day further up the Misty Fjords, the weather was a lot better and I was heading for another cabin. The cabins in the area were rented out and you had to book them in advance but I figured it would be silly to camp
outside if they were empty. Plus it felt like "sticking it to the man." After my treatment by the authorities that sounded good.

Got some fishing done on my way and caught a big Coho. This time there was nowhere to land it as the channel had vertical cliffs on each side so I had to pull it into the kayak. So using the small net and some hocus-pocus I got it in.

The cabin was on an Island called Winstanley. There were a lot of sightseeing boats and floatplanes going past. The Misty Fjords was a popular area. On approaching the cabin it was apparent that there were people staying there; there was a boat moored up and some kayaks on the beach. There were two groups, a family staying in the cabin and a group of girl kayakers from Sitka. The girls directed me to a camp spot behind them. The girls were a group of friends who got together every year for a kayaking trip, and it was great swapping stories with them. I shared the salmon and we sat around chatting the evening away.

There was a ban on fishing in the area that I did not know about, so they advised me to keep quiet about my fish. But since it was already caught it would be a shame to waste it.

One of the girls slept with a shotgun for the bears. I didn't think she would ever need it, but I could see the value of her sleeping better with it. Just hoped the bear wouldn't be sniffing around my hammock when she shot at it!

The family in the cabin were from Ketchikan but were a bit shy and kept to themselves. The girls however had just been to the place I was heading, Punchbowl Cove, and told me about a trail up to a lake with two rowboats I should check out. It sounded great and I couldn't wait to get a proper hike in the wilderness. They said the day was that good when they hiked up they skinny-dipped and dried on the rocks up there.

They were heading off the next morning and

insisted on giving me their leftover candy and cheese. I'm not a big candy eater but on this trip I had massive cravings for it and sweet stuff. In Ketchikan I had bought 12 donuts for six bucks and ate them in about two hours, in total I ate 36 donuts the whole time I was there (two days) so their candy was much appreciated. And being seasoned kayakers, they knew what to bring; small snacks to nibble on as you kayak. I nicknamed them the Sitka/California babes as one was from California. They were real good people and I was glad I had met them. It was the only time I had shared with other kayakers on the water and it was good to talk about the different aspects of kayaking, like to follow the coast very close as it seems like you are moving faster or just cut across big openings where it must be quicker but seems like you are getting nowhere.

But they had to go and so did I. Their boat came and picked them up and they headed off. The girls said it was not far and I thought I would make it in about four hours so I was in no hurry.

I could see why it was a popular area. The Granite Mountains started in the ocean and just rose straight up. It was an awesome site and I kayaked most of the time looking up.

The campsite in Punchbowl Cove was right beside a massive granite wall but it was misty so I couldn't see all of it. I spent the afternoon setting camp but it was back to raining again and I didn't want to do the hike to the lake in the afternoon in case the hike took longer and I got stuck.

There was not a lot of wood around I could use for a fire as everything was very wet and I had to work at getting to the dry stuff, so fires were small. I set off for the lake early the next morning and it was a steep hike with a big waterfall to the side of it. But there had been a storm that spring which led to a landslide, and to clear the path the US forestry department just used dynamite to blast the fallen trees out the way! It made a right mess.

There were some old papers in the cabin at Alva and reading them I discovered it's illegal to buy beer, sell beer, or brew your own in some parts of Alaska. I would bet money it's easier to buy dynamite than it is to buy beer in Alaska.

As I made my way up the trail I got to the top and could see the start of the lake. It was my first real hike into the woods. On my trip there just was not anywhere to go most of the time and I was in a hurry to get to Alaska. So I was sure I would see some awesome wildlife and I crept on my tiptoes with camera in hand to the lake. Although it was eerily quiet there was bugger all wildlife, but the views were fantastic. A lake surrounded by giant granite slabs with misty surroundings. I took one of the boats out for a spin but there was not much to look at. The mist had descended and closed in.

There was no wonder I didn't see any wildlife, every 15 minutes a floatplane would buzz by and if it was clear they would go as low as they could. There was no chance of me skinny dipping as it was too bloody cold, and anyway I had a shower only four days ago I was still good for a few weeks.

When I got back down to camp there was a yacht in the bay and the people came ashore. They were four old codgers sailing around the Alaskan islands that stopped off for the hike up to the lake. I was a bit concerned as the trail was not good and it was getting late but they only came to check it out for doing it the next day.

They came back ashore the next day and it was pouring rain. I pointed them in the direction but I didn't think they would get up the trail as it would be nasty. But they seemed determined to give it a shot and were also seasoned hikers so I was sure if it was too hard they would have the sense to turn around, which they did. Well, two of them found it too treacherous and headed back, so they invited me out of the rain to the yacht for a sandwich and tea. That was great as I was bored stiff and there was bugger all to do; the rain was bucketing down.

They were two Americans and two New Zealanders who had sailed and hiked all over the world. It was good listening to their stories. I got the feeling they were not too interested in my kayak trip, which was fine with me. I was keen to find out where they had been and if there were any hidden hot springs about. Sadly the only hot spring was quite far for me to get to and they did not find it when they looked. The storm in the spring had done a lot of damage to the trail.

I got a lift back into the shore and just hid from the rain in my hammock. The next morning the yacht just headed off. I thought they might say goodbye, but nope.

The weather was crap again and I just didn't have the motivation to head out, but instead did some fishing in the cove as now the ban was lifted. I only caught small Rockies and threw them all back. Later that day I was in for a big surprise a boat came in with about eight kayaks on the back and started unloading them in the water and ferrying them to shore.

It was a college student group from North Carolina, two professors and about eight students. Wow that was different for me! I decided to hang around as they wanted to explore the fjords and I was keen to actually kayak with people! Their plans the next day was to kayak deeper into Punchbowl Cove and get picked up by the boat for the return trip. So I was going to go along with them halfway and come back and do some fishing.

That morning having breakfast was interesting. There was a girl on the beach with another girl over her shoulders doing squats, very entertaining! The girls in the group were doing their morning exercises.

Paddling with a group was different. It took so much longer, everybody wanted to look at everything, but they were taking lots of pictures and I thought that would be a nice change. I had to leave them to their trip and headed back to do some fishing as I hoped to catch some fish to add to whatever they got out of their crab traps. I spent the rest of the day fishing but it was not good in this area for some reason. I only managed to catch four decent sized fish but did get two Red snappers, which I was delighted with!

The boat came back and a load of them went up to the lake to skinny dip and I helped check the crab traps. I was fair chuffed with my catch of fish but the boat captain and his helper had been fishing all day and got a lot better haul than mine, he even got a small Dog shark. I was not impressed with the captain at all. He made some cuts in the shark and used it to rebate the crab traps, but the fish was still alive and I believed there was no need. He also filleted the fish alive. I don't mind killing animals to eat but I object to making them suffer for no apparent reason. I liked to watch people fillet fish so I could learn, but his technique was terrible. He left most of the good meat on the fish and we had to remove a lot of the bones he had sliced through. The professor onshore filleted my fish and got the maximum out of the fish. I was really impressed. It was a real good job and if you're going to eat an animal in the wild I believe it's very wrong to not try and use as much of it as you can.

So we had loads for the pot that night and the students made a lovely meal out of it. One of the girls had a very sharp eye and after dinner she noticed a bear and cub by the river. We all went over for a wee look and I was amazed at how small the mother bear was. It seemed as it was no bigger that a big dog. I had expected to see an abundance of wild life on my journey but it was few and far between.

I was just getting my water from the river and boiling it and sometimes on the trip I would just drink it straight from the rivers just as they did at some of the communities I had visited on the trip. They did it at Namu, and Lou did it at Butedale, and as a boy I remember our hikes in the Scottish Border hills drinking from streams with my cousin Eddie and my uncle Eddie.

But the professors were adding bleach to their water, which I could not get my head around at all. I believe that you can't hide away from bugs and if you try to, when you do get hit by them you will be hit hard as you will have no tolerance set up. Plus out in the wild drinking bleached water didn't appeal to me whatsoever, but each to his own. There are plenty of arguments to say I'm crazy for drinking straight out of the streams!

It was a good change having lots of people around but they were due to head back the next day and I was going to make my final push for the border. I gave them a hand to get their stuff into the boat in the morning and said goodbye. They were a good bunch and really brightened up my stay in the Mistys.

I was lucky; it was a good morning. There was even some blue sky peeking through the clouds. I headed back to Winstanley Island hoping the cabin would be empty as I could do with drying out.

But as I got there it was occupied. This time by three guys out on a trip in the wild, but luckily for me they were just waiting on a plane to come and pick them up. They said the cabin was booked for another couple of nights by them and I was welcome to it, which was great!

Got talking to them and they were blown away with my trip. They had thought they were pushing the boat out getting flown out here and staying in a remote cabin for three days.

The floatplane came in and I helped them load up, talking to the pilot from Ketchikan. After he heard my story of heading to the border as I was told to get out of America he offered to strap the kayak to his plane and drop me off right on the border. I wasn't even tempted by the offer it would feel like cheating if I got a lift.

I don't like cheating on anything even if nobody is ever going to find out it doesn't matter I would always know! I wanted to do the trip under my own steam. Plus I calculated my trip would be over 1,000 miles if I paddled back so that was an added bonus. When the guys took off the pilot circled around a small island and buzzed down low right over my head, it was pretty cool!

I had the cabin to myself and it was time to dry out and relax. I chopped some wood and settled down in the cabin drying out all my clothes. I planned on getting going early the next morning but little did I know I would still be there three days later as a storm moved in. Those days were totally and utterly boring but I was glad I had somewhere to hide out. The wind and rain battered the place for three days only letting up for an hour or so before the wind brought in more rain. If I had gone out in it I imagine it would be like the movie "The Perfect Storm" and I would be riding 30 foot waves!

All this extra time spent hanging around was using up my supplies fast. After three days of it there was a break in the weather and I knew that it might not last but I had to make a break for it. I kayaked down to the main channel and on my way I saw movement on a beach by a small river. It was the biggest bear I had seen on my trip, walking along the beach, so I turned the kayak to investigate and as I was getting close the bear started running. I was still far off shore and couldn't understand why the bear was running off. There was no way he could see me and be scared. Then I noticed the pack of wolves running down the river and onto the beach. There were seven of them, all chasing
the bear. The bear leapt into the forest and the

wolves stopped at the trees and just about turned and trotted down to the shoreline and lay down. It was like this was their patch and the bear had been vanquished so everything was back to normal. These wolves were a lot healthier looking and a lot bigger than all the others I had seen. As I got close they disappeared into the forest but I don't think it was because of me. It was certainly an unexpected bonus. There has never been a documented case of wolves attacking and killing a human in North America; probably because they don't leave any evidence behind! They are smart cookies and even the bears don't mess with them. As I got further down towards the main channel the wind picked up and I ended up battling my way to a safe sheltered bay. However, the storm was back and I was stuck, as outside the bay it was terrible. I spent a further two days stuck there and in the course of it I lost all my fishing lures and snapped my rod in half. There were lots of whale bones on the beach and I found what I guessed was a whale tooth. This was a disaster. I was running low on food now and it looked like there would be no fishing as well.

The weather eased off and I got out but I was going to have to make some good distance as I didn't know if the bad weather was over yet.

I was passing my old campsite where I forgot to pick up the glass ball I found so I decided to stop off and get it.

The ball was exactly where I have left it. Picking it up had altered my course slightly, so, on my way again. As I paddled I noticed a boat passing and suddenly change course my way. They introduced themselves as a bunch of kayak fishermen and they had a camp further up and Howard invited me for dinner! This was awesome.

I had not expected to meet anyone else on my final dash to Canada. Howard run a kayak tour company out of Ketchikan for the tourists and two weeks every summer he takes out some hard-core kayak fishermen to this place to fish for the big halibut. It was great meeting the guys. They were from all over America, from New Jersey to Seattle. I had heard of kayak fishing but these guys took it to a whole new level. The kayaks were great and one even had pedals and went just as fast as paddling but seemed effortless. Dinner was tasty. They had their own cook and a great setup. Talking to the guys and hearing about their fishing trips was great and they all thought I was a wee bit crazy and I was getting a lot of respect for what I had done. These guys were some of the best kayak fishermen in the

US and I was amazed at what you could catch from a kayak. Howard had caught a 300lb marlin that towed him 11 miles out to sea over five hours. I was gobsmacked. The next day they were taking the morning off to go visit a river with the salmon running up, which I had not seen yet so I tagged along. It was a nice kayak up the estuary as the tide was coming in and the feeling of heading up the tight channels surrounded by trees made you feel like you were going somewhere special and the banter with the guys was great.

Got to the river but the salmon were not running like you see in the documentaries but there were big groups of them and the guys liked playing about trying to catch them. Running salmon don't feed but will bite a lure out of habit. They just can't resist! I was surprised we didn't see any bears. I thought this would be prime bear area but I suppose from what I know of bears now that the ones in the real wild are very shy of humans and probably scattered when they smelled us.

I was planning on just heading away on my trip after but with all the talk about these guys pulling up 60-70 pound halibut from the kayaks and fighting monster marlin I had to see it!

So I decided to stay one more night and go out with them on in the evening. Wow, they were pulling up monster halibut and boy was it tricky unhooking them. They had caught so much the first day that they had enough for their food. They only landed enough to feed themselves and the rest went back to live another day. For these guys it was all about the sport and they gained a lot of respect from me.

It was great to see how they pulled up the real big ones by working together. They would join up to hold the kayak steady and give the fisherman more leverage, but unhooking these monsters was a dangerous thing. The hook could easily pop out at high velocity and into the de-hooker. The big fish were really powerful and could whip their heads with real force. It would have been much easier to just cut the line but like all good fishermen retrieving your favourite lure is imperative; those things are like gold.

I got Danny from New Jersey to keep a big Red snapper for me to take away on my final final push for Canada the next day.

These guys knew how to fish and loved the sport. Sitting in a kayak and fishing is the way forward. This was the highlight of my trip. It was a real unexpected treat, the experience of sharing these guys' trip for a short while, and the great attitude of the guys was exceptional.

That night was their last night also and they had a few beers that needed to be drunk so we sat up drinking them. It was a good crack and the only time I had stayed up late the whole trip. It's just not the same by yourself; you soon get bored. Of course, drinking beer makes you pee, so as I was going down to the ocean to pee off the rocks for the first time I was seeing the bioluminescence created by the plankton. It was the most interesting pee time I have ever had in my life; making swirls and patterns with your pee is highly entertaining.

We didn't stay up too late as the guys wanted to get a last fishing session in before they headed off the next morning. That morning Dave introduced me to his energy boosters, pancakes rolled up with jam and peanut butter in them, and Danny had an old pair of neoprene gloves he didn't want and was going to throw out if I didn't take them. These two things were very important and going to have a very big impact on my day, I would go as far as to say they saved my life!

It was great bumping into the guys like that and the cook was amazing and the food was awesome!

Chapter Five
Danny the Champion of the World

As I headed off, the weather was not the greatest but reasonable, I needed to make it around Dixons Pass. Coming up had been easy and I had seen plenty of beaches I could stop on if it got rough, so I didn't mind heading off in slightly dodgy weather.
As I headed out it got steadily rougher but I was well rested and fed so I just kept going. I got out of the bay and into the full swell. It was okay and I could manage it. Then the weather deteriorated very fast. I started looking for shelter and a beach to land on but the waves were too big and directly hitting the beaches. So I kept going as I was sure I had seen plenty on the way up and all I needed was a beach pointing away from the waves.
I soon got to what I thought was the halfway point and to go back was as hard as going forward, so there was no turning back. The weather changed gear again; all the beaches I had seen on the way up were behind pillars of rocks that looked easily navigable in calm weather but treacherous in the current weather. The swell was revealing hidden rocks that were

exposed as the waves sucked up the water and when the waves hit the rocks they would explode 30 feet into the air. There was no way I was going to risk navigating them and even if
I did get through them I would have to surf a big wave onto the beach. Getting off the beach would be just as bad if the weather didn't get better, so I could end up stranded. So my only option was to keep going.
The wind, rain, and swell made it very interesting paddling. My hands were freezing even with Danny's gloves on. If I hadn't had them I think I
would have been in real trouble and would have had to risk landing, which I figured would end in disaster nine times out of ten. I found it amazing that on the day I would need proper gloves somebody gave them to me. Looks like I still had Forest Gump's feather and the planets staying lined up!
The kayaking in that weather was what I would call reactive paddling, you had to be ready all the time. There was no slacking off. Your strokes had to match the big waves and you had to keep at the right angle because you didn't want to be heading straight on to them or you would be thumping up and down, and you definitely didn't want to be side on or you would be capsized before you could say "shit."
As I looked at the waves to judge my strokes, I noticed something horrifying in the distance; there were monster waves up ahead. Worst of all they were not consistent, they just appeared out of nowhere in sets of three, and then there would be nothing. These rogue waves had me real worried.
What if there were more and I was in them? I

would have no chance. I had to be ultra-alert to everything around me, and I watched the area for the big waves. Luckily I had noticed them in plenty of time and managed to see that they started very far out. There was no way to judge when they would come through and how long I would be in the area, so I was going to have to go far out around them. I was in awe of their awesome power. They would start out at a slightly different angle to the rest of the waves and grow till they consumed all waves and kept building to a high point, then the tips would start turning white and then they would thunder into great giant monsters consuming everything in their path until they smashed into the rocks. It was like the "Jaws" theme tune where it would build up and up and up and up then bang!

I was uncomfortable going so far out but had no choice. I saw a fishing boat further out and was wondering what they would have thought if they could see me.

I got around the monsters and kept my eye out for more but I was getting tired. There was no stopping for lunch and I had eaten all my daytime paddling snacks a long time ago. I had also underestimated the distance and still had a long way to go before safety. I had been reactive paddling for eight hours and I was incredibly tired and had to really focus to keep alert. The weather eased off a bit and I could see the end, I just had a few rocks to go round to get to a safe beach, just in time, as it was starting to get dark.

Landing on the beach, I pulled myself out of the kayak onto very wobbly feet. Relief, I had made it! Although I didn't look for the day's events I had a sense of accomplishment. I had taken everything the ocean could throw at me and survived. There had been a feeling of disappointment growing on me through the trip. At the start I perceived the trip I was about to do to be physically and mentally hard and I would be challenged to my limits. If it had not been for the constant rain it would have been a very easy trip and even with the rain there was no part of the trip that I believed anybody could not do. This was a day that made the whole trip for me. It took all my stamina and strength, and a lot of composure. I had been challenged and had been taken to my limits, something in me changed this day, my confidence and belief in myself went through the roof!

I didn't have a lot of time as it was getting dark quick. I set up my hammock and got cooking. Boy was I hungry; I fried up the Red snapper and devoured it. The guys gave me a big block of salami too so I chopped some up and chucked it into the rice with some cheese, wow, that filled me up!

Planned on doing a long video diary update about the day but was way too tired and hit the sack.

Amazingly enough, the weather the next day was good, which was a relief as I had a big crossing to do. As I paddled past the same spot where I caught the Steelheads on the way up I did some fishing with the broken rod and a lure one of the fishermen (Bill) gave me. I caught a Steelhead straight away and as it was lunch time, decided to land and cook it up just over the border into Canada. Got some dry wood from under a big fallen tree and covered the salmon in tinfoil. While it was cooking I made a garlic, cheese, chicken stock sauce. You can't get much fresher fish than 30 minutes from water to fire and it tasted fantastic!

Since it was a nice day I decided to cut a corner off my trip that made the crossing two times bigger and took forever. I didn't find a place to camp till it was dark and had to move very quickly. I started a fire first and then set my hammock up in the woods. By the time I was all sorted and fed it was near pitch black, and as I headed to the hammock that was just behind a big tree from my fire, I disturbed a bear sniffing around my gear. He got as big a fright as me and took off into the woods as I shouted at him, although he didn't go far before stopping and turning around to look at me. I could just see his eyes staring at me. I picked up some stones and threw them at him and got my torch out of my pocket and shined it at him, which got him going. I stayed there shouting like a loony throwing stones for about five minutes after he had gone, just to make sure!

I was very tired. It had been another big day and allowing the bear to keep me up during the night was not an option, so I moved the fire near my hammock and stocked it well.

I was too tired to let it bother me and slept well. I had noticed when I was setting camp that there was a lot of rubbish lying around and the next morning I saw the full extent of it. No wonder the bear was investigating and seemed brazen, there was litter everywhere. It was an island but just across the bay was a native town Lax Kw'alaams and I take it the kids used this spot as a camping area and didn't bother cleaning up after themselves.

I grew up in the country and closing farm gates behind you and taking your rubbish with you was just how it was done.

Natives get a lot of flak in North America for being drunk, lazy, messy, and living off the government, but trust me it is the same all over the world. You can find just as many if not more Scottish, English, French people doing the exact same thing and a lot worse in some places. I think that when governments dish out free money you will get people who abuse it or believe they deserve it. In my opinion it is easily solvable; the money and help should still be there but people should work for it, doing projects that improve their community (like picking up litter). Ah, the solo kayaker's life is great. There is never anybody to point out the

flaws in your ideology!

Getting near communities was reminding me at how my trip was coming to an end and I would have to settle back into real life! The thought of settling back in was a bit scary and for ninety per cent of the trip had not been on my mind. After my troubles with US Customs I was dreading dealing with the Canadian Customs.

Technically I had overstayed my holiday visa by quite some time, but there was no record of me coming into Canada so how could they prove I did? But also I was skint. My plan was to sell my kayak and travel back to Vancouver and pick up some casual work to fund my departure. However, I could not tell them this could I? And they would likely want to see funds, and I'm the worst liar.

The US Customs needed me to report in to Canada before the 31st of August or I wouldn't be allowed back into the USA ever.

This was all playing on my mind. There was a

good chance of them deporting me. If the weather hadn't been so bad I think I would have just kept kayaking down the coast.

I set off from the island and all day I was trying to work out my best course of action. It ended up another long day but I got back to an old camp site of mine on a wee long island which was only a four hour kayak to Prince Rupert, where I figured I was just going to have to take my medicine and face up to the consequences of being a slightly sketchy character. Last night camping and I savoured it. Whatever happened next I had enjoyed myself and had an experience that would last with me forever.

I got up early and headed to Prince Rupert. It was a fitting day; cold, wet, and miserable, I had heard from people on Oona River of a good hostel in PR where I might be able to swap some work for my stay. I had all my fingers and toes crossed for this.

I only had around 90 bucks to my name. Pretty good going for 10 weeks, as I only started out with $290 and had a $200 boost from my brother. If you calculated the cost of the fresh seafood I had consumed over the trip for nothing, I was probably up 1,000 bucks.

I stopped off on an island to have a last camp meal before I headed into PR just in case the US Customs had phoned ahead and I would be collared as soon as I set foot in PR. Then like a condemned man I headed in I kayaked all the way along the docks looking for somewhere to park the kayak, and everywhere wanted money. I thought what do they think I am in, a bloody pleasure craft?

I found a place that let me park up as long as I moved it that afternoon, and I got to wash up in their toilet, which I knew from my last encounter with civilisation I needed!

I went looking for the Pioneer Hostel and found it just up the road. I went in and spoke to the owner Christy. I explained my situation and asked if I could work for my stay, She asked me what I could do and I told her my background in general construction. It turned out as I came into the hostel she was having a discussion about a drainage problem in the basement. It was perfect. I could sort it out for her no problem. This was a big relief. As I went to pick my kayak up and bring it to the hostel I looked all over for signs saying you must report to the Customs and didn't see any. I decided there and then I was willing to forfeit getting back into the US and not going to go out my way to declare myself as last time it turned out so bad. This was a massive weight lifted off my shoulders and all I had left to do was sell the kayak. That couldn't be hard on a coastal town could it?

For the next few days I sorted out the drainage problem and bought myself two kilograms of meat for making burgers, and I ate burgers for lunch, dinner and supper, I was in Heaven! There were a lot of donuts consumed also.

I was sitting in the front room one afternoon and a guy came in with a load of camping gear with a rather wild look about him. Turned out he had just solo kayaked from Vancouver! His name was Chris and he was from New Zealand. We hit it off straight away.

To begin with, I took one look at him and thought he was mad. Then we got talking about equipment and kayak experience and it soon became obvious to me that if he was mad, I must be of been absolutely off my rocker!

His equipment and experience were vastly superior to mine, and he thought he was a bit sketchy till he met me. It was good talking to someone who had just been through the same stuff. I could not have landed in a better place to readjust to normal life, Ju the hostel manager was a fun excitable German girl who brightened up everyone's day. Chris and I decided to try and sell our kayaks together as he had the same plan as me. Just as we were sitting down to think who could buy our kayaks, in walks a small Japanese guy with a big backpack and a paddle. I looked at Chris and we both went No! But yup, turned out he kayaked from Vancouver to Glacier Bay north of Juno in a foldable kayak!

Chris and I couldn't believe it; he could hardly speak English. His name was Minoru but we nicknamed him Ripper as he had done his trip really quick. He had got past the border trouble I had by jumping on the ferry from Prince Rupert to Ketchikan and on his way back he got off the ferry at Ketchikan and paddled down to Prince Rupert completing the route. It was funny how we all met up in the Pioneer Hostel in the same week after leaving Vancouver all at different times, and all having our own very different ways of doing the trip.

Swapping stories, Chris and I noticed we both had stopped on the same island coming around Cape Caution, the island where I had the bear come sniffing about my hammock in the middle off the night. He had stopped there as it was on his "inside passage guide book" but had only spent five minutes there as there were massive Grizzly bear paw prints on the beach! I was like hold on there is a book?

I still had my beard from the trip and I was not going to shave until we sold the kayaks just in case the trip was not finished! We were really struggling to sell them but after two weeks we sold them to a really nice couple from an Island out of Prince Rupert. We managed to sell them for 1,500 bucks. Chris had bought his new but it had taken a beating on the rocks. It was plastic like mine but it was two-toned so the scratches came out a different colour and they looked worse than they were. We split the money 600-900 and decided to hitchhike back to Vancouver together. We made a lot of friends in the Pioneer Hostel and Prince Rupert. Chris was an avid rock climber and he found a local guy, John, to take us out climbing. John lent me some gear and they taught me to climb on Copper Mountain in Terrace. I was hooked on climbing within five minutes, I had tried it before indoors but the climbing gym was far from me so it never took off but this outdoor climbing on real rock was a different story, I was having visions of a whole new adventure!

The couple that bought our kayaks tried to lend us their car to go exploring BC, but Chris and I were like "you don't understand we are totally unreliable sketchy dudes; you can't give us your car!" The people in PR were fantastic but after our journeys with all the rain, we were a bit jaded and probably not the greatest at talking about our trips. You soon get fed up at answering all the same questions and some people treating you as if you're amazing. It was a relief when people didn't care and were not interested.

I loved the hostel environment but I was still a bit sketched out with the outside world my inner hermit was refusing to die quickly and I refused a few invites to dinner and party's.

We set off on the Highway of Tears to Vancouver, and the first question out of Chris's mouth every time we got a hitch was, "So why is this called the Highway of Tears?" I just shook my head and sat quiet as they explained lots of people go missing on it.

We parted company at Catch Creek as Chris was heading to Squamish to climb and I needed to get to Vancouver.

I settled in Vancouver and two months later started to watch the video footage of the trip. I thought it would be torture watching it again but I ended up really enjoying editing it into a watchable video. I was amazed it ended up being 2 hours and 37 minutes long. I made it so friends and family could watch it back home and posted it on YouTube. I made a joke at the end saying I was saving all the other stories that happened off camera for the book, as anybody who knew me would know I hate writing. People are lucky to get a Christmas card from me and even then it will be as simple as I can make it! But after it took off on YouTube, lots of

people started commenting on when the book would be out and that brought me to here….

Afterword

Since the trip lots of people have asked me if the trip changed me, and for a long time after I would reply with yes it had but nothing felt real different. In my eyes there was nothing special about what I had done, Lots of people kayak the inside passage it's no big deal.

When I edited the video footage and realised it was over two hours long I was shocked. I then put it up on youtube expecting a few friends and family to watch it. But then complete strangers watched it and started commenting how much they enjoyed it.

After about 6 months of getting great comments from complete strangers and friends, I did start to feel different. Over the years I had perfected the art of appearing like a confident person but really I had little confidence in myself.

I was starting to feel real positive about myself and what I could achieve. I did not put this down to the trip more to the people who had put big smiles on my face with their complimentary comments. After a while there were a lot of people asking about the book and friends were asking why not.

My experiences with writing were bad I did not like it, and the thought of writing a book seemed like a real crazy idea. However the new found confidence in me said why not give it a bash what have you got to lose?

So in secret I started to write, instantly was blown away with how much I enjoyed it! It had never occurred to me that I would enjoy it. Every night after work I would add some writing and relive the trip. As I relived it I could remember everything as clear as day and lots of things that I had totally forgotten about came to me. I have always enjoyed reading and always hated writing but that was before I realised the power of writing your thoughts and memories down. I found myself walking alone the street and smiling at some of the moments I had on the trip. Like coasting in the kayak closed to the foe deer on the rocky bank and the feeling of euphoria at the Mark's Cabin. Now when people ask me if it's changed me I can honestly say yes. It didn't happen with a bang but the trip planted a seed and from it a great big tree grew.

I also get asked a lot even straight after the kayak trip what's my next adventure as if my life is constant crazy adventures!

I have responded to this with a few ideas but nothing concrete. One idea is to attempt the North West Passage, this has not been done in one season yet and my eyes light up at the thought I could be the first to solo kayak it in one season. It would take a real kayak and planning and a lot of training but I believe it is possible. I have thought about it a lot and looked in to the different challenges; the biggest stumbling block is as always money.

I would like to thank you for reading about my wee adventure and hope you enjoyed it as much as I have writing it.

I would also like to thank all the people who

helped me get into the water and the people on my trip.
Some people deserve a special mention who helped me with the book Lisa Duthie, Annie Anemone and Kristie Amadio

Cheers Danny

In case you didn't notice I named the chapters after some of my favourite books, The Lion the Witch and the Wardrobe (CS Lewis), The Power of One (Bryce Courtney), The Old Man and the Sea (Earnest Hemingway), Insomnia (Stephen King), Danny the Champion of the world (Roald Dahl).

This is me
Copyright: Danny Wilks
Published 1st February 2013
Publisher Danny Wilks